Shakespeare, Jonson, and the Myth of Venice

View of Venice in *Civitates Orbis Terrarum* (1593), by Georg Braun and Frans Hogenberg. From Huntington Library Call Number 180544. By permission of The Huntington Library, San Marino, California.

Shakespeare, Jonson, and the Myth of Venice

David C. McPherson

DELAWARE
Newark: University of Delaware Press
London and Toronto: Associated University Presses

Associated University Presses
440 Forsgate Drive
Cranbury, NJ 08512

Associated University Presses
25 Sicilian Avenue
London WC1A 2QH, England

Associated University Presses
P.O. Box 39 Clarkson Pstl. Stn.
Mississauga, Ontario
L5J 3X9 Canada

The paper used in this publication meets the requirements of the American National Standard for Permanence of Paper for Printed Library Materials Z39.48-1984.

Library of Congress Cataloging-in-Publication Data

McPherson, David C., 1935–
Shakespeare, Jonson, and the myth of Venice / David C. McPherson.
p. cm.
Includes bibliographical references.
ISBN 0-87413-397-1 (alk. paper)
1. Shakespeare, William, 1564–1616—Knowledge—Italy—Venice.
2. Venice (Italy) in literature. 3. Shakespeare, William, 1564–1616. Merchant of Venice. 4. Shakespeare, William, 1564–1616. Othello. 5. Jonson, Ben, 1573?–1637. Volpone.
I. Title.
PR3069.I8M28 1990
822.3′3—dc20 89-40722
CIP

PRINTED IN THE UNITED STATES OF AMERICA

For Fran

Contents

Acknowledgments

Colleagues here at the University of New Mexico and at other universities have helped make this a better book by reading the manuscript and offering valuable suggestions. Particularly, I want to thank R. B. Parker, George Arms, Mary Bess Whidden, Richard Helgerson, R. L. Montgomery, Jr., Beth Bartolini-Salimbeni, Juliette Cunico, and James Thorson.

Also helpful were the dedicated librarians at the Biblioteca Marciana in Venice, the British Library in London, and the Huntington Library in San Marino.

Finally, I thank the regents of the University of New Mexico for granting the sabbatical leave that made it possible to do the research on which the book is based.

Shakespeare, Jonson, and the Myth of Venice

Introduction: Urbs et Orbis

> . . . orbis, non urbis esse forum quispiam non ineptè diceret
>
> (Someone said not ineptly that [the Piazza of San Marco in Venice] is the forum not of the city but of the world)
>
> —Stephanus Pighius, *Hercules Prodicius* (1587)

Renaissance Venice was both a city and a world. Like many Elizabethans, William Shakespeare and Ben Jonson were clearly fascinated by that world. In *The Merchant of Venice, Othello,* and *Volpone* the playwrights make inspired use of both the local color and the symbolic values of *La Serenissima Repubblica.* No other extant English plays before 1642 contain any really notable uses of the city.[1] But Shakespeare's and Jonson's brilliant evocations of Venice have of course been studied before. Why a new study now?

The best reason is that recent historians have made great strides in more precisely defining what values Venice symbolized for sixteenth- and seventeenth-century Europeans. They have shown that certain aspects of the city's reputation became so powerful that, in the aggregate, they may justifiably be called the *Myth* of Venice, and that England was the country in Northern Europe in which this *Myth* was most strongly felt.[2] Here I want to make the insights of the historians more readily available to students of literature, but I also use those insights to examine the plays themselves.

I have profited not only from the recent contributions of historians but also from those of literary scholars, particularly Gail Kern Paster's *The Idea of the City in the Age of Shakespeare.* It provides a broad ideological framework into which my study of a specific city fits.[3]

Another important reason for this study is to make extensive use of certain sixteenth-century sources in Italian, French, and Latin. Scholarly opinion seems to be swaying toward the idea that both playwrights could read those languages.[4] My study is not heavily dependent upon the idea that they could, since we have a lot to learn about how they used sources on Venice that were available in English; but much is gained by assuming that both could have referred to some of the standard Venetian histories and guidebooks in those three languages. The assumption is risky, but it opens certain lines of inquiry unavailable to those who have been more cautious.[5]

There is also value in studying the two men's uses of Venice together instead of separately as most critics have done. A century or so ago, Bardolaters did make the comparison, but only in order to exalt Shakespeare at Jonson's expense. In *Volpone,* Karl Elze claims, Jonson "lays the local colouring on inches thick, but it is everywhere the work of a bookworm. . . . Jonson may do what he likes, the greater the effort he makes the less he deceives us. . . ."[6] In scorning "the barren and unpoetical learning of a Jonson," Elze is apparently unaware of the irony in the spectacle of a study-bound scholar damning a poet for relying on the study. Shakespeare's Venice, by contrast, was said by another Elze—Theodore this time—to be "not the product of poetic invention, but a mirror of reality."[7] In contrast to these Bardolaters, I start with the assumption that Jonson's use of Venice, though very different from Shakespeare's, is at least as powerful—if not more so.

A minor reason for a new study is that there has been too great a tendency to talk about the Elizabethan image of Venice as if it were identical to the Elizabethan image of Italy as a whole.[8] Venice was a very special place, and attitudes toward it were different; I have tried to take this fact more fully into account than previous scholars.

A word about English history versus Venetian history: many scholars have assumed that the Venice that we encounter in these plays is, for the most part, a disguise (some would say a *thin* disguise) for London; and therefore they have used English, not Venetian, history, as background.[9] While I would be the last to deny that much has been learned in that way (with, doubtless, more to come), I believe that Venetian history should be consulted also. Because the Myth of Venice has been neglected, I concentrate here almost exclusively on the Venetian side of things. But that does not mean that I consider English history irrelevant.

I do, however, take issue with those who think the Venetian references are superficial at best. Shakespeare's geography may not be detailed (there is never a mention of a canal, for instance); but I am convinced that he not only knows but uses the main outlines of the Myth of Venice, and even some of the minute details which appear to be erroneous may not be entirely so.[10]

The plan of this book is as follows. The first chapter treats the question of where Shakespeare and Jonson might have gotten their facts and ideas about Venice. The second outlines the Myth of Venice, with more attention to the darker sides of the city's reputation than most historians have given (some refer to these darker sides as the "Counter Myth"[11]). The next three chapters deal with elements of the plays that are better understood against background provided by the Myth, with each play getting its own chapter. The conclusion provides a very brief comparison of the two playwrights' uses of Venice.

* * *

Bibliographical note: all quotations are given in English; for passages that I myself have translated, the original is provided, normally in the footnotes. My policy in quoting Renaissance sources has been to normalize "i" and "j," "u" and "v" and silently expand abbreviations. Signatures are given for books published up to 1650, page numbers for those published thereafter. Diacritical markings are not always found in sixteenth- and seventeenth-century Italian books; for consistency I have silently supplied a few, the absence of which might have caused confusion, in accordance with modern Italian usage. I have, however, left such marks as are in the originals—whether they are used in modern Italian or not. Readers unfamiliar with the standard abbreviations for journals specializing in English literature should consult the Table of Abbreviations at the beginning of the notes.

Venice, Western Half, 1566. Note the reverse "S" of the Grand Canal, upper center, and the Piazza di San Marco, with all its famous buildings, extreme right near top. All canals, churches, and notable sites are given numbers on the map and explained in a verbal key below. This system enables anyone who has access to the whole map in unreduced size to identify the specific locations mentioned in *The Merchant of Venice, Othello,* and *Volpone* (e.g. the Rialto, Ducal Palace, Procuratia, Arsenale, Lazaretto, Scrutineo, Piscaria, hospital of the Incurabili, and monastery of San Spirito). The engraver was Bolognino Zaltieri. By permission of the British Library.

1
"I had read Contarine": Sources for Shakespeare and Jonson

Sir Politic. Within the first week of my landing here
All took me for a citizen of Venice,
I knew the forms so well—

Peregrine. [*Aside.*] And nothing else.

Sir Politic. I had read Contarine, took me a house . . .

—*Volpone* 4.1.37–40

Facts and ideas about Venice were available to Shakespeare and Jonson in profusion. Here I will not be arguing that either playwright necessarily used a particular source; rather, I will be demonstrating how many *kinds* of possible sources were available. These were both oral and written.

One possible "source" (and this is stretching the term) would have been personal observation of the city. But we have no evidence that either playwright ever went to Venice, and it seems highly unlikely that either did. The lack of evidence has not prevented a few Shakespearean scholars from speculating, however. Karl Elze, whose quaint views have already been quoted in the introduction, asserts: ". . . if any supposed journey of Shakespeare can be made probable, it is above all the journey to Italy."[1] Citing some instances of accurate Venetian local color in *Merchant,* Elze concludes (inaccurately, as I shall show): ". . . the disbelievers in an Italian journey of Shakespeare cannot account for his knowledge by any other means than that of oral communication."[2]

A quarter of a century later Lewis Einstein was just as impressed by Shakespeare's knowledge of Venice, but not at all impressed by his knowledge of the rest of Italy. Hence he offers the hypothesis that Shakespeare had been a sailor on an English merchant ship that had made port at Venice. This theory, says Einstein, would "account for his partial knowledge of Italy, coupled with its gigantic blunders; it would explain both his fondness for Venetia as well as much of the mystery surrounding his early life."[3] But good sense had already begun to prevail. In the same year in which Einstein was offering these speculations, another scholar says forthrightly: "To the question whether Shakespeare ever visited Italy a negative is the only reply to be made."[4] The cycle continues in more recent times. In 1961 A. C. Partridge was still proposing the journey, and responsible scholars such as Mario Praz and Samuel Schoenbaum were still showing how unlikely the theory is.[5]

Though the Venetian local color is more extensive in *Volpone* than in either of Shakespeare's Venetian plays, the idea of a Jonsonian journey thither has been suggested rarely, if at all, probably because the documented connections between Jonson and John Florio, to be discussed later, make any such hypothesis seem unnecessary.

I. Kinds of Possible Oral Sources

Through the years the most frequently mentioned kind of oral source has been, with good reason, the returned traveler, merchant, diplomat, or student. Such men must have been fairly numerous around 1600. The Pope complained to the Venetian authorities in 1593 and again in 1595 about the number of English heretics in Venice.[6]

Many English noblemen and gentlemen had traveled there but did not publish descriptions (for example, Sir Philip Sidney).[7] Once regular and elaborate diplomatic contact resumed in 1603, one must consider returned members of the ambassador's staff. For instance, Nathaniel Fletcher, brother of the dramatist, was one of Wotton's chaplains in Venice in 1604–1605; and John Fletcher and Ben Jonson were presumably good friends.[8] As for returned students, the University of Padua had long been popular with the English as George B. Parks notes.[9] In the late 1580s, the English traveler Webbe counted thirty English students there.[10] The modern historian, John Walter Stoye, argues that the intelligent Erastianism of the Venetians made Padua a good university for foreigners—especially Protestants. He contends that Anglo-Venetian relations were probably improved by ties between returning English students and the Venetians with whom they went to school.[11]

Along with Englishmen returned from Venice, Venetians also resided in London. For instance, we know from documents relating to the Gunpowder Plot that Jonson was in contact with a chaplain of the Venetian ambassador in November 1605—just about the time that he was writing *Volpone.*[12] In addition, the Italian expatriate community in London was sizable.[13]

II. Possible Oral and/or Written Sources: A Hybrid Category

Many English travelers wrote down their impressions of Venice, but the manuscripts were unpublished at the time that our three plays were written. Hence the playwrights could have heard versions of these travels from the mouths of the authors (or of the authors' friends), or they could have read the accounts in manuscript. A distant possibility in this category is the colorful narrative of Sir Thomas Hoby, the translator of Castiglione's *Courtier.* Although Hoby died in 1566, it is faintly conceivable that Shakespeare or Jonson somehow came across his manuscript.[14] Fox, a servant to Henry Cavendish, is chronologically a more likely source, having been to Venice in 1589.[15] Likelier still is Fynes Moryson, uncle of the Sir Henry for whom Jonson wrote the Cary/Moryson Ode. Although Moryson's narrative was not published until 1617, it describes a journey to Venice in 1593–1594. He was in London off and on during most of the years in which the plays were probably being written and thus could have served as an oral source; but his manuscript may also have been penned already and hence is a possible written source.[16]

In addition there were in London professional middlemen, mediating between Italian and English cultures. In this category I place John Florio, a naturalized Italian, and Lewis Lewkenor, an Englishman born. Both men could have served Shakespeare and Jonson as oral as well as written sources, although it seems that neither middleman had ever actually been to Venice.[17]

Florio's connections with both playwrights have been thoroughly studied.[18] That Florio served Jonson as an oral source for *Volpone* is almost certain because of the inscription in a British Library copy of the play: "To his loving Father, & worthy Freind Mr. John Florio: The ayde of his Muses. Ben Jonson seales this testemony of Freindship & Love."[19] The Earl of Southhampton provides a link between Florio and Shakespeare: he was patron to both in the early 1590s. Florio has even been mentioned as a prototype for Holofernes.[20]

Another good possibility (and more interesting because less thoroughly discussed) is Lewis Lewkenor. His *Commonwealth and Government of Venice* (1599), in part a translation of Gasparo Contarini's *De Magistratibus et Republica Venetorum* (Venice, 1543), was published in time to have served as a source for both *Othello* and *Volpone;* and scholars agree that it is indeed a minor source for both plays.[21] But Christopher Whitfield has argued, with some plausibility, that the treatise may also have been a source for *The Merchant of Venice.*[22] Given the usual dating of *Merchant* (1597), this necessitates the theory that Lewkenor served Shakespeare as an oral source or that Shakespeare read the manuscript.

The manuscript is not known to have existed that early; but there is evidence, both internal and external (and not adduced by Whitfield), that it might have. The internal evidence is strictly negative: there are no events described therein that took place later than 1585. In that year Doge Nicolò da Ponte died and Pasqual Cicogna was elected. Lewkenor records these events. Cicogna himself died in 1595, but Lewkenor does not mention this fact in his thumbnail sketches of the lives of the Doges. Lewkenor's tourist-oriented material does not mention the impressive new stone Rialto Bridge that replaced the old wooden structure in 1591. The external evidence is biographical. Lewkenor speaks in his preface of periods of enforced idleness that drove him to pen and paper. This stretch of years was probably in the mid-1590s when he published his other works,[23] and is unlikely to have been after 1597, when he was settled in his family's property and elected to Parliament.

The difficulty with a mid-1590s composition date for *The Commonwealth and Government of Venice* is that the preface speaks as if the work had been commissioned by Lewkenor's patroness, Anne, Countess of Warwick; and it is hard to explain why—if it was a command performance—he kept it by him so long. Whitfield's own somewhat tortured evidence in favor of the notion that Shakespeare used Lewkenor in *Merchant* is biographical, but of a different sort from mine. He tries to show that Lewkenor and Shakespeare moved in some of the same circles (the Inns of Court, the Royal Court), and therefore that they might have been acquainted. All in all, the idea that Lewkenor was a source for *Merchant* should be regarded as interesting, possible, but far from established.

III. Kinds of Possible Written Sources

1. POSSIBLE SOURCES IN ENGLISH

First to be considered here are books in English that deal primarily with history and government. The first of any importance is William Thomas's *History of Italy* (1549). It reached a second edition (1561) and may have retained some reputation because it was Protestant. Francesco Guicciardini's *History of Italy* was translated by Geoffrey Fenton and published in 1579. Jonson himself owned a copy of the second edition, 1599.[24] A source not normally thought of in such a context as this is the memoirs of Philippe de Comines, translated by Thomas Danett (1596). Shakespeare or Jonson might have found mildly interesting not only Comines's own remarks about Venice but also the footnotes on Venice by Danett. Lewkenor's translation of Contarini, already discussed, was of importance in forming the very favorable view of the Venetian constitution which prevailed in England during the seventeenth century.[25] Finally in this category, Richard Knolles's *History of the Turks* (1603) was a minor source of *Othello,* as several scholars have noted.[26]

Englishmen with a serious interest in Italian culture began by learning the language, and so the various dictionaries and language manuals in English or English/Italian are likely sources too. For instance, Florio's *Second Fruits* (1591) is one place Shakespeare could have picked up Holofernes's proverb "Venetia, Venetia."[27] And I have no doubt that Florio's aid to Jonson's Muse in *Volpone* consisted not only of oral assistance but also of his Italian/English dictionary *A Worlde of Wordes* (1598).

Shakespeare, but not Jonson, almost certainly used collections of Italian novelle in English, especially Painter's and Fenton's.[28] These stories do not often use Venetian settings, but those that do seem extraordinarily interesting for my purposes here—especially Painter's version of Bandello's "Two Gentlewomen of Venice," to be discussed in detail in the *Othello* chapter.

Also in English were several geographical reference works, some of which were also intended as tourist guide books. George Abbot, for example, published in 1599 his *Briefe Description of the Whole Worlde* (second ed., also 1599; third ed., 1600; fourth, 1605). Robert Johnson's translation of Giovanni Botero's *Relationi universali* is the same sort of book as Abbot's. It came out in 1601 under the title *The Travellers Breviat* and again, revised, in the same year, under the title *The Worlde,* and finally (for my purposes) in 1603, again revised, under the title *An Historicall Description.*[29]

Useful to potential tourists were the accounts in English of voyages to Venice and the pamphlets of advice to young travelers. Unlikely to have been used, because published so long before, were the travel narratives of Sir Richard Guylforde (1506) and Andrew Boorde (1542).[30] Much more plausible as a source is *A Direction for Travailers* (1592), listed as being by Justus Lipsius but much of it by the translator Sir John Stradling.[31] Although Lewkenor's *The Commonwealth and Government of Venice* is usually listed as a translation of Contarini, it is far more. It contains excerpts from five authors besides Contarini, and the excerpts make Lewkenor's book useful not only to students of government but also to prospective tourists—which means that it contains details on the city potentially useful to dramatists.

2. POSSIBLE SOURCES IN OTHER LANGUAGES

Either Shakespeare or Jonson—one thinks particularly of Jonson—could have used Lewkenor as a kind of annotated bibliography.[32] The five works other than Contarini from which Lewkenor prints excerpts in English would all have been helpful to a dramatist provided he had wanted to take the trouble to find and translate them. Both dramatists would have doubtless preferred sources in English, but the idea that they might have used Lewkenor's "bibliography" is not at all inconceivable.

Lewkenor's first set of excerpts are from Donato Giannotti's *Libro de la republica de Venetiani,* first published in 1540. Giannotti, a Savonarolan Florentine, was a great admirer of the Venetian government even though his friend Machiavelli was not. His book would have been easily available because it was so often bound with—even printed with—Contarini's.[33] A man with Jonson's scholarly bent might well have sought out the original Contarini just to see if Lewkenor was translating well, and in seeking out the original might have found Giannotti between the same two covers.

The second of Lewkenor's subsidiary authors is Bernardo Giustiniani, a fifteenth-century humanist noted for his eulogistic history of his native city.[34] Giustiniani's Latin would have proved little barrier to Jonson; and Shakespeare could surely have done it too, if he had wished to. Third on the reading list I am hypothesizing is Sebastian Münster, a geographer whose reference book, first published in German in 1544, quickly appeared in a Latin edition (1550). He has a good map of the city of Venice and much other information besides.[35]

Münster's handsome folio served well enough for the study, but the tourist on the move needed a small, lightweight octavo guidebook. Such a book began to appear about 1561 and was reprinted numerous times, usually under the title *Delle cose notabili della città di Venetia.* Francesco Sansovino takes credit for authorship in the 1561 edition, and he probably deserves it.[36] *Delle cose* treats such subjects as the history of women's fashions in Venice (Sig. B2 ff), prostitution (B4v), marriage customs (B5), painting, sculpture, and architecture (C8v), festivals (E5v), churches (E7), the famous Arsenal (E8), *et cetera.* Discussions of the Venetian government (for example, Sigs. I3–I7) are far outweighed by other kinds of tourist information.

Finally Lewkenor borrows from an even more thorough tourist manual—this one indisputably by Sansovino—*Venetia città nobilissima* (1581). Here Sansovino includes the same sort of material that is in *Delle cose,* but in much greater detail. For example, we get not merely a list of every church and monastery but also a minute description of their art and architecture.[37]

Dozens of works on Venice's history and government other than those used by Lewkenor had been published in Italian, French, and Latin in time for Shakespeare and Jonson to have seen them. Machiavelli, Jean Bodin, and Pietro Bembo had all published relevant works; and all three men are mentioned by name in the text of *Volpone.*[38] Would Jonson, with his pride, have dared to mention their names without having some knowledge of their works? Most were available in Latin too (see previous footnote). Jonson does not mention the Piedmontese author Giovanni Botero by name, but does use in *Volpone* a phrase which is also the title of one of Botero's recent works: *Ragion di Stato* (Venice, 1589). Since the phrase was common, the connection is by no means certain. A few of Botero's other works were translated into English. In addition to *Relationi universali,* there was *Delle cause della grandezza della città* (1596), translated 1606.[39]

Jonson may also have used Florio's extensive library of Italian books, which are listed individually in the front matter of the middleman's *A Worlde of Wordes* (1598), Sig. B4v. The library includes a good many works of fiction, poetry, and drama.

Most of the non-English works discussed so far are much likelier sources for Jonson than for Shakespeare; but the reverse is true of Italian novelle, whether in Italian or French. We scarcely need to be reminded that neither the main source of *Merchant* in *Il percorone* nor that of *Othello* in *I hecathommithi* has yet been found in English. If Shakespeare read these stories in Italian or French, why not others in the same and similar collections?[40]

Additional reference works in foreign tongues might have proved useful. Such works are usually well indexed, and so it would not have been necessary to plow through reams of paper to find what was needed. For instance, there was Leandro Alberti's *Descrittione di tutta Italia.*[41] Franciscus Schott's little manual in Latin (1600), which is silently indebted to Alberti, was published in Antwerp, closer to London. Schott is also indebted to Stephanus Pighius's *Hercules Prodicius* (Antwerp, 1587), which contains an especially vivid section on Venice.[42]

In the sixteenth century several French tourists published accounts of their visits to Venice, but the only one readily available to Shakespeare and Jonson is that of Jacques de Villamont, whose book was first published in Paris in 1595; its availability would have increased by its republication there in 1596 and at Arras in 1598 and again in Paris in 1600 and 1604, to name only the editions published early enough for these three plays.[43]

Maps form another kind of source available to Shakespeare and Jonson. Detailed maps of the city had been published both as single sheets (see, for instance, the one by Bolognino Zaltieri) and as part of a huge collection of city maps (the one by Georg Braun and Frans Hogenberg).[44]

Last I want to mention Cesare Vecellio's *De gli habiti antichi, et moderni di diverse parti del mondo* (Venice, 1590, 1598). In it are more than sixty woodcuts of modern Venetian social types in their proper costumes. Facing each woodcut is a commentary on that particular social type—in Italian in 1590, in both Italian and Latin in 1598.[45] These commentaries go far beyond costume. Here we find such types as magistrates, Sig. N8v, 1590 ed. (cf. Jonson's Avocatori), senators, Sig. N7v (cf. Shakespeare's Brabantio), Commandatori, Sig. P5 (cf. Volpone's disguise in Act 5), and a Doctor of Laws from the Veneto, Sig. V5v (cf. Portia's disguise). Busy playwrights would surely have appreciated the visual aids provided by the woodcuts. Women's fashions are given more space than men's, which suggests that this costume book was probably created mainly for women. Pictured are women of all social stations from gentlewomen to prostitutes. Both pictures and commentary pertain to the various female characters in all three plays.[46]

* * *

Four Venetian social types. Pictured here are a Venetian senator (such as Brabantio in *Othello*), an advocate (such as Voltore in *Volpone*), a magnifico (such as Volpone in *Volpone*), and the commander-in-chief of the Venetian military in wartime (such as Othello in *Othello*). From Abraham de Bruyn, *Omnium . . . Gentium Habitus* (Antwerp, 1581), Plate 32. By permission of the British Library.

Sources of many kinds, then, were available to Shakespeare and Jonson. They did not necessarily use them, but they certainly could have. We turn now to the various shapes of the Myth of Venice that the playwrights would have encountered in these different kinds of sources.

2
Venetia, Venetia: The Myth of Venice

> *Holofernes.* I may speak of thee as the traveler
> doth of Venice:
> *Venetia, Venetia*
> *Chi non ti vede, non ti pretia.*
>
> —*Love's Labour's Lost* 4.2.97–98

The proverb quoted by Holofernes is printed in a mangled form in both the quarto and folio texts of *Love's Labour's Lost.*[1] We cannot be sure whether the mangling is due to Shakespeare making fun of the Pedant, to the playwright's own errors, or to the vagaries of compositors. In one respect, however, I like to think that Shakespeare was making fun of his character: in a source likely to have been used by the dramatist, there is another part to the proverb: *"Ma chi ti vede, ben gli costa."* Florio translates "Who sees not Venice cannot esteeme it, / But he that sees it payes well for it."[2] Holofernes, I suspect, is heaping praises on Venice but ignoring the city's drawbacks.

Just as there were two parts to the proverb, one complimentary to Venice and the other not, similarly one finds always in the sixteenth and seventeenth centuries both bright and dark sides to the city's reputation. Here I want to examine both the bright and the dark sides of four components of the Myth of Venice: Venice the Rich, Venice the Wise, Venice the Just, and *Venezia-città-galante.*

These categories are either identical or similar to those of various historians, but most have been adapted for my purposes here. Franco Gaeta's seminal article distinguishes three elements of the Myth: "We can speak of a myth of Venice the mixed state, of Venice the state of liberty, and of Venice the city of pleasure" (*"Venezia-città-galante").*[3] A mixed state was thought to be the ideal form of government, and Venice was regarded as having just the right mixture. The political wisdom of the Venetians was also considered validated by the fact that the Republic had never been conquered ("Venice the state of Liberty"), and an aspect of *La Serenissima*'s political wisdom was said to be its extraordinarily impartial and severe justice. Gaeta gives little attention to *"Venezia-città-galante,"*and when he does he alludes mainly to the times of Casanova.[4] But another historian, Oliver Logan, uses Gaeta's term to refer to Cinquecento and Seicento Venice as well as Settecento Venice, though he too downplays the importance of it.[5] To Shakespeare and Jonson, however, Venice as pleasure capital was one of the most crucial elements of the Myth; hence I give it far more prominence than any of the historians on whom I am relying. For "Venice the Rich" I base my ideas chiefly on the work of Brian Pullan, an economic historian.[6]

I. Venice the Rich

In the time of Shakespeare and Jonson, if one used only one adjective to describe Venice, it was almost always "the Rich." *A Direction for Travailers* is typical: ". . . in *Italy* of late *Roome* is dubbed the great, *Florence* the faire: *Naples* is called the Noble, and *Venice* is christened the rich Citie."[7] The city's publicists boasted that it was "the most copious and rich city under the heavens,"[8] a "terrestrial paradise."[9] Outsiders used a lot of hyperbole also, especially tourists: Canon Pietro Casola, for instance, a Milanese with no axe to grind, who passed through on his way to the Holy Land in 1494 writes:

> . . . I must make my excuses to the readers of this my itinerary, if it should seem to them that I have overpraised this city of Venice. What I write is not written to win the goodwill of the Venetians, but to set down the truth. And I declare that it is impossible to tell or write fully of the beauty, the magnificence or the wealth of the city of Venice. Something indeed can be told and written to pass the time as I do, but it will be incredible to anyone who has not seen the city.[10]

One of the favorite symbols of Venetian wealth and hence favorite subjects for travelers' descriptions was the Treasury of Saint Mark. The following lengthy quotation from Franciscus Schottus conveys the atmosphere of opulence so prominent in Volpone's opening speech to his gold and in his seduction speeches to Celia:

> . . . wherein are twelve pretious Crowns, with twelve Brest Plates, all compassed about with fine Gold, and garnished with many Stones of great value. Among divers others, with *Rubies, Emeralds, Topasses, Crisolits,* and other pretious Stones, and Perls of unmatchable bigness; Two Unicorns Horns of a great length, with a third somewhat less. Many very large Carbuncles [cf. Jonson's "Carbuncle able to put out both the eyes of our Saint Mark"], Vessels of Gold, Scollops of Agat, and Jasper Stones of a good bigness. One Huge Ruby given this State, by *Domenico Grimani,* a most worthy Cardinal. An Emerald hower-glass heretofore presented to this most illustrious Seigniory, by *Uscassano* King of *Persia,* with many other pretious things, Vessels, and Censores of Gold, and Silver. There also lies the Mitre or Bonnet (as we call it) with which every new Duke is Crowned. The which is traversed all over with the finest Gold, and pollish't, in whose wreathes, are many most pretious stones; and at the very Top, a Carbuncle of inestimable valew . . . .[11]

Everyone knew, of course, that the main source of Venice's wealth through the centuries had been its trade with the East; thus Salerio accurately imagines Antonio's cargo as consisting of spices and silks *(Merchant* 1.1.33–34). Paolo Paruta, one of Venice's official historians (chosen by the Senate), discusses the city's origins:

> . . . there was not any City famous for merchandizing in the *Levant,* whither the *Venetian* Ships and Merchants did not flock. . . . through whose hands the most precious Merchandise of those Countries past, to the great advantage of the City, and of her private Citizens.[12]

As a modern historian has said, the Venetian nobles before the sixteenth century were traders: "They could not trace their descent from any landed class, but felt themselves no less noble for that."[13]

In order to maintain this trading empire the Venetians had to create a military empire as well, and this power also fascinated visitors. The Arsenal, whose managers were "probably . . . the greatest direct employers of labour in Christendom,"[14] was the visible symbol of this might; and descriptions of it were just as obligatory as descriptions of the Treasury of Saint Mark. According to a favorite tale of tourists, this huge arms factory and military base built and fitted out an entire galley in a day while a delighted Henry III of France watched.[15] Manufactured were such items as ropes, crossbows, and pistols. In a huge warehouse there the Venetians kept vast stores of gunpowder (which blew up in 1569, the noise allegedly heard forty miles away; Jonson's Sir Politic Would-be seems to be aware of this event).[16]

Venice's economic and military power made it a magnet for foreign traders, and the resulting cosmopolitan atmosphere became part of the city's legend: "One sees in this city an infinite number of men from different parts of the world, with diverse clothing, who come for trade; and truly it is a marvelous thing to see such a variety of persons, dressed in diverse habits."[17] Sansovino notes that the Piazza di San Marco is frequented by "Florentine, Genovese, Milanese, Spanish, Turkish, and other merchants from different nations of the world."[18] Giacomo Franco's engraving of the crowd listening to a mountebank labels its pictures of various nationalities, and includes an Englishman along with a Greek, a Frenchman, a Spaniard, and a Turk.[19] A French traveler comments: ". . . if you are curious to see men from all parts of the world, each dressed in his different mode, go to the Piazza di San Marco or to the Rialto, where you will find all sorts of persons."[20] Münster sums up Venice's reputation for both riches and cosmopolitan atmosphere:

> In sum, this superlatively magnificent, beautiful, and rich city has become Queen of the Sea, and is inhabited by huge throngs of people of various races, indeed from virtually all nations, come together in that place to trade.[21]

Of the many dark sides of Venetian wealth and power the one that interests me here is the widespread perception in the sixteenth century that this wealth and power was in decline. Some modern historians have disputed this traditional notion,[22] but for my purposes the real state of Venetian economic affairs around 1600 is not so important as what Europeans of the time believed to be true. The discovery in 1499 by the Portuguese of the sea route around Africa was widely believed to have cut deeply into Venetian wealth.[23] Other Renaissance observers attributed the alleged decline to the seemingly inexorable advances of the Turk into territories formerly Venetian—the most notable of which, for students of *Othello,* was their conquest of Cyprus in 1571. In 1538 DuBellay wrote a famous sonnet which wittily makes the point about the Turks. He names all the glories of Venice—for example, the Piazza, the Rialto, the Arsenal—and

Return of the Doge from the ceremony of marriage to the sea. The ceremonial Buccintoro, in which the Doge rode, is accompanied by a huge number of other vessels. From Giacomo Franco, *Habiti d'huomeni* [*sic*] *et donne Venetiani* (Venice, c. 1609), Plate 18. By permission of the British Library.

then, in closing, alludes to the annual ceremony in which the Doge "marries" the Adriatic:

> Mais ce que 1'on en doit le meilleur estimer
> C'est quand ces vieux coquz vont espouser la mer,
> Dont ilz sont les maris, et le Turc 1'adultere.[24]
> (But that which you must find does best adorn her
> Is when those cuckolds old go wed the sea.
> Venetians husbands then, the Turk the horner.)

Abbot mentions both the Portuguese *and* the Turks:

> The impoverishing of their [i.e. the Venetians] state, hath partly beene by the encroching of the Turke: but especially By the decaying of that trafique which they had to Alexandria in Aegypt for their spices, and other riches of Persia, Arabia, and the East Indies. Since the course of the Portugals to those Easterne countries hath beene by sea, by the backeside of Africa.[25]

II. Venice the Wise

In addition to riches Venice was renowned for political wisdom. As the most successful and long-lived of modern republics, it was much admired by most political thinkers with republican tendencies. Traiano Boccalini, for example, in his witty *I Ragguagli di Parnaso* (1612), has this chapter heading: "Sebastian Veneri, *Duke of* Venice, *after his admittance into* Parnassus, *desires* Apollo *that he may have the precedency given him before Hereditary Kings and Monarchs; and obtains a favourable Decree from his Majesty.*"[26] Villamont explains the connection between wisdom and political success: "For the laws of wise and prudent men are the soul of the Republic."[27] Another French observer, Pierre d'Avity, follows Contarini in seeing the Venetian constitution as composed of elements of all three of Aristotle's kinds of government: the one (the Doge), the few (the Senate), and the many (the Grand Council). The Venetian state, he sums up, ". . . is composed of all the three kinds . . . out of which they have made one that is perfect."[28]

Venice's panegyricists tried to show that the Republic's political wisdom included a genuine love of peace. Paruta, for instance, is surprised that Venice did not grow into a greater empire sooner, but says their tardiness ". . . ought not to be imputed to the baseness nor wretchlesness of her Inhabitants but rather to their Modesty: For the custom of our fore-fathers, was not to undertake War out of a desire of Rule; but to preserve their Liberties. . . ."[29] In later ages, however, other nations (Paruta continues) envied Venetian prosperity; and hence in self-defense, the Venetians had to expand their territories and armed forces(!). Lest we be too skeptical, however, a study by two modern historians claims that this idea has "like other aspects of the Myth, a core of truth."[30]

The political wisdom of the Venetians was thought by many to be validated by the sheer longevity of the Republic. Contarini propounded the legend that it had existed essentially unchanged since its supposed founding in 421 A.D. Less partisan students of politics, like Jean Bodin, pointed out that there had in fact been significant constitutional changes in the long history of the Republic; but Contarini's view largely held the field. We would expect Paruta to support the official view that Venice's longevity is proof of its political wisdom, and he does (*Politick Discourses*, p. 123). But admirers from other nations chimed in. James Howell, one of the "Sons of Ben," has a list of a dozen reasons for the Republic's durability: for instance, she is constant to herself (that is, consistent and conservative in government and institutions), more inclined to peace than war, the people are less volatile than those in other parts of Italy, they are patriotic, and so forth.[31]

The favorite metaphor for the Republic's longevity was Venice as Virgin. Writer after writer identifies her preservation of her liberty (freedom from domination by a foreign power) with sexual chastity. Porcacchi uses it in a pamphlet which Jonson might have come across.[32] Boccalini imagines Argus offering to guard Venice's chastity; but this offer is turned down, being judged an unnecessary precaution (p. 88). The virginity metaphor was a particular favorite of English writers. Lewkenor points out that it ties in with the idea of the Virgin Queen—thus allying (at least metaphorically) *La Serenissima* with England:

> . . . the rest of the whole world honoreth her [i.e. Venice] with the name of a Virgin, a name though in all places most sacred and venerable, yet in no place more dearely and religiously to bee reverenced, then with us, who have thence derived our blessednesse. . . . (Sig. A4)

Howell's prefatory poem in *S.PQ.V.* is somewhat charming in its optimism and naiveté (and execrable verse):

Upon the Citty and Signorie of *Venice.*

Could any State on Earth Immortall be,
Venice by Her rare Government is She;
Venice Great *Neptunes Minion,* still a *Mayd*
Though by the warrlikst Potentats assayd;
Yet *She* retaines Her *Virgin*-waters pure,
Nor any Forren mixtures can endure;
Though, Syren-like on Shore and Sea, Her Face
Enchants all those whom once She doth embrace;
Nor is ther any can Her bewty prize
But he who hath beheld Her with his Eyes:
These following Leaves display, if well observed,
How She so long Her Maydenhead preservd,
How for *sound* prudence She still bore the *Bell;*
Whence may be drawn this high-fetched parallel,
Venus and *Venice* are Great Queens in their degree,
Venus is Queen of *Love, Venice* of *Policie.*
(Sig. B4v)

The metaphor of virginity still had imaginative force at the sad end of the Venetian Republic, although Wordsworth's famous sonnet makes a melancholy contrast with Howell's poem:

On the Extinction of the Venetian Republic

Once did She hold the gorgeous east in fee;
And was the safeguard of the west; the worth
Of Venice did not fall below her birth,
Venice, the eldest Child of Liberty.
She was a maiden City, bright and free;
No guile seduced, no force could violate;
And, when she took unto herself a Mate,
She must espouse the everlasting Sea.
And what if she had seen those glories fade,
Those titles vanish, and that strength decay;
Yet shall some tribute of regret be paid
When her long life hath reached its final day:
Men are we, and must grieve when even the Shade
Of that which once was great, is passed away.[33]

Observers often attributed the longevity of Venice to its political unity. To make the point, Botero (not a Venetian) contrasts Rome and Venice by saying that one speaks of the accomplishments and victories of the Romans as individuals (for example, Julius Caesar did this, Scipio did that): "But in the history of

Venice one sees the reverse; . . . one says that the Venetians have done this or that, not this or that individual."[34] Some modern historians agree that Venetian society was relatively unified. Early in this century Molmenti, perhaps drawing on Botero, contrasted Florence and Venice:

> At Florence a few individuals . . . dominate history. . . .At Venice . . . the individual was absorbed in the State, which refused independent initiative to the individual. . . . The ambitions of the Medici would have found no fitting soil in Venice. . . . As in public life, so in art. . . .As a rule . . . in Venetian pictures the individual is lost in the joyous throng.[35]

McNeill accepts the idea of "the cohesion achieved among the citizens of Venice" and attributes it in part to "the isolated, insular location of their city."[36]

The late seventeenth-century writer Amelot de la Houssaye sums up the connection that was thought to exist between the Republic's longevity and its unity: ". . . the great reason why they . . . lasted so long under one Government, was their Citizens knowing so well how to obey. They are very secret and close. . . . They are People of great Order, Providence and Judgment."[37]

The dark side of a reputation for political wisdom is a reputation for craft; and of a reputation for peacefulness, cowardice in war. Canon Casola, though a tremendous admirer of Venice, nevertheless writes of Venetian gentlemen: "For the most part they are . . . astute and very subtle in their dealings, and whoever has to do business with them must keep his eyes and ears well open" (pp. 143–44). Bodin is much more cynical and censorious; he thought the latitude allowed the people of Venice a deliberate piece of craft: ". . . to make them more mild and pliable, they give them full scope and libertie to all sorts of pleasures."[38]

A reputation for being peace-loving is always double-edged in a macho world. Fynes Moryson believes the Venetians to be cowardly vis-à-vis the Turks: "And indeed the Gentlemen of Venice are trayned upp in pleasure and wantonnes, which must needs abase and effeminate their myndes."[39] Bodin remarked that the Venetians were "better citizens than warriors."[40]

Unity, too, has a dark side. The price of it, to some observers, was suppression of individual freedom—a true "Big Brother" situation. Etienne La Boetie inaccurately takes the Venetians to task for surrendering their primitive liberties to the Doge; while Francesco Vettori, a friend of Machiavelli, more accurately blames the patriciate: "Is it not tyranny when three thousand patricians hold sway over one hundred thousand persons. . . ?"[41] An aspect of Venetian unity which drew much unfavorable comment from foreigners was the Republic's refusal to allow citizens much contact with outsiders. Montaigne, who visited the city in 1580–1581, said that if a gentleman spoke twice to him, the Signiory would hold that person suspect.[42] The same objection was raised a century later by Maximilien Misson and Saint Didier,[43] the latter noting that Venetian nobles were forbidden any dealings even with servants in a foreigner's household. Boccalini attributed much of the Republic's success to the ability of noble Venetians to keep state secrets (p. 41–42), but the price of their power was a certain amount of suspicion in the air at all times.

III. Venice the Just

Part of political wisdom is, of course, justice. But Venice had such a special reputation for justice; and Shakespeare and Jonson made such important uses of the reputation of Venetian justice, that this subject deserves separate and extended examination.

Venetian justice was thought to be different, partly because "they use not as in other places the civil law [in the sense of Roman law], but live and are governed by their own laws and peculiar course of justice."[44] Lewis Lewkenor claims, ". . . there was at one instant threescore sundry Ambassadors from severall princes and commonwealths in *Venice,* desiring to have such controversies as were among them ended and decided by the Senate, such was then the fame of the uncorrupted justice of the Fathers" (Sig. Ff2^{v}). Giustiniani traces the origin of the high esteem in which justice was held to a sort of Golden Age of the forefathers:

> . . . there was among them the deepest concord and a great love. All things were had in common, the private held as public, the public as private. From this it necessarily followed that justice was most highly honored.[45]

The greatest fame Venetian justice enjoyed was for its supposed impartiality, even toward the lower classes and outsiders—which is, of course, what Shylock was counting on. Bodin, who did not have a high opinion of the Venetian constitution, nevertheless praises the impartiality of the judiciary system highly

(McRae, ed., p. 785). Boccalini tells a colorful anecdote which illustrates well this aspect of the Myth:

> . . . some Plebeians in *Venice*, being gon according to their custom, to the Sea-side to sollace themselves with some young Courtisans which they had carried along with them, they were so beaten by some Noble Venetians, as the former betaking themselves unto their swords, slew one of the others, and handled the rest but ill. For which fault, being sent for by the Judges, those Plebeians, although they saw all the Judges in the power of the offended Nobility, yet they hoped so much in the uprightness of the Senat, and in the exact Justice of the Tribunals for offences, as they stuck not to make their appearance, and go to Prison: Nor were they deceived in their opinion; for the Judges finding by the defence which they made, how they had been molested by those Noble Venetians, they were as innocent, set at liberty, to the eternal glory of the uncorrupt Venetian Justice. (p. 13)

The Venetian diarist Sanudo noted down his pride in a judgment in favor of a Florentine against a Venetian patrician.[46]

In addition to its vaunted impartiality, Venetian justice was praised frequently for its severity. Swearing was sometimes punished in laymen by the loss of a hand, tongue, or eye.[47] In 1609 the Scottish traveler Lithgow watched a friar burnt alive for lechery.[48] Moryson saw two young sons of senators have their hands cut off at one of the sites of their mischief, their tongues cut out at the site of their singing of blasphemous songs, and finally their heads chopped off by a sort of guillotine in the Piazza.[49]

The highly favorable image of Venetian justice had definitely reached England. Lewkenor hyperbolizes, ". . . their justice is pure and uncorrupted: their penall Lawes most unpardonably executed" (Sig. A2^{v}). The same two points (impartiality and severity) were still being made by Venetian partisans early in our own century. Molmenti, with astonishing naiveté for a modern historian, asserts that "legal procedure was at all times marked by spotless honesty and perfect equanimity," adding a few pages later, "But if Venetian justice was purer than elsewhere, it cannot be denied that it was remarkably severe."[50]

Of course there were those in the sixteenth and seventeenth centuries who were not impressed by Venetian justice. Contrasting sharply with Boccalini's anecdote is Sir Thomas Hoby's anecdote about a fray that occurred when he was in Venice in 1549. A foreign count and a Venetian magnifico both wanted to dance with the same woman, and a shoving match ensued. The Venetian tried to stab the foreigner, but the latter was wearing a coat of mail. The foreigner then drew his rapier, and was felled by the sword of one of the Venetian's retainers. Hoby adds, "There was no justice had against this gentlman [*sic*], but after he had a while absented himself from the citie the matter was forgotten" (p. 14). William Thomas notes that ". . . corruption (by the advocates' means) is so crept in amongst the judges that poor men many times can want no delays in the process of their matters" (pp. 77–78). Amelot de la Houssaye attributes the severity of Venetian justice to ulterior motives:

> They have a great vanity to be thought good Justiciaries. . . . But there are two things generally complained of in their Judicature; One is, that few of them are versed in their Laws. . . . The other, that upon any Offence they condemn People to the Galleys, as well for trifles as for the greatest Crimes, according to their interest, that is, to their Necessity for Rowers: and this is the reason why so few People are Executed, neither are they more scrupulous for Banishment, and Confiscation of Estates. For there needs not much reason of *State* against those who are rich. . . . (p. 281)

The severity of Venetian justice offends modern readers. The loss of hands, tongues, or eyes for swearing seems to us especially barbaric. Torture, too, was common. The Officers of Night (see *Othello* 1.1.182) were said by Canon Casola to employ in their hearings "the torment, called in our tongue the *Curlo*," or, in English, the rack (p. 126). Hoby mentions that a nobleman guilty of premeditated murder was tortured but not put to death: "But for all they putt him to the torment of the cord, they coulde never make him confesse. . . . And the law is, except a man confesse his tresspace when he is putt to this torment, he shall never suffre deathe for yt" (p. 16).

IV. *Venezia-città-galante*

Despite the dark sides of Venice the Rich, Venice the Wise, and Venice the Just, the European image of these components of the Myth was, generally speaking, more often favorable than unfavorable. The same cannot be said of that aspect of Venice's reputation which historians have dubbed *Venezia-città-galante*; here, the image was dark—or perhaps one should say lurid, with the darkness visible.

Nevertheless, there certainly was a bright side. Venice was the pleasure capital of Europe, and many of these pleasures were legitimate ones. Tourists flocked in, then as now, to see the beauties of *La Serenissima*. Lewkenor notes that while travelers "of a graver humor" are struck by the "greatnes of their Empire, the gravitie of their prince, the majesty of their Senate, the unviolablenes of their lawes, their zeale in religion, and lastly their moderation and equitie," by contrast "some of the youthfuller sort, would extoll to the skies their humanitie towardes straungers, the delicacie of their entertainments, the beauty, pomp, and daintines of their women, & finally the infinite superfluities of all pleasure and delightes" (Sig. A2). Canon Casola expresses an idea which has occurred to most tourists in Venice, regardless of century: "Though I wished to see everything, I saw only a part, and even that by forcing myself to see all I could" (p. 129).

Even in the time of Shakespeare and Jonson tourism was a major source of revenue for the Venetians, and they worked hard at pleasing foreign visitors. In the early sixteenth century, an English traveler, Sir Richard Torkington, comments gratefully:

> Ther I was well at ese, ffor ther was no thyng that I Desyred to have but I had it shortly. At Venyse, at the fyrst howse that I cam to except oon, the good man of the howse seyd he knew me by my face that I was an englysshman. And he spake to me good englyssh, thanne I was Jo[yo]us and glade, ffor I saw never englyssh man ffrom the tyme I Departed owt of Parys to the tyme I cam to Venys . . .[51]

In the interests of balance I should point out that not all tourists were keen about Venice, and among those less than enthusiastic were two famous names: Michel de Montaigne and Sir Philip Sidney.[52] Late in the seventeenth century, Richard Lassels sums up, from a tourist's viewpoint, the defects of Venice:

> Having thus seen all *Venice*, over and over againe, in amonths [*sic*] stay there, I was most willing to leave it; having found it true of *Venice*, what *Socrates* sayd of *Athens*, that it was *melior meretrix, quam uxor*; a fine towne for a fortnight, but not to dwell in alwayes; and this, by reason of some *stinking channels; bad cellers* for wine; *worse water*; and the *moist ayre of the Sea* not the most wholesome; *scarcity of earth* even to bury their dead in; and *little fewel* for fireing. So

> that findeing the four elements wanting here in their purity, I was willing to leave. . . .[53]

But for every dissatisfied or half-satisfied tourist, there must have been a hundred who were enthusiastic.

What, then, were some of the legitimate pleasures that drew all these tourists to Venice? Besides admiring the general beauty and magnificence of the city's architecture, art, bridges, and canals, many were drawn to Venice by the civic pageantry and holiday revelry—not only annual events but also special occasions. Molmenti asserts: "In Venice of the sixteenth century luxury and splendour surpassed all bounds; never before at any time nor in any city were religious ceremonies, victories, . . . visits of foreigners . . . celebrated with greater pomp and magnificence."[54] The historian Edward Muir has recently devoted a whole book to civic ritual and its functions in Venetian society.[55]

Among the annual events the most spectacular processions and celebrations were at Carnival, Ascension, and Corpus Christi. Carnival at Venice predictably featured masquerading, dancing, and attending comedies. Sansovino comments:

> And in the Fontico de i Tedeschi it was customary in the three days before Carnival to make a public feast with open doors, where all the masked figures of that season came together in a continual dance, which lasted all three aforesaid days. Also held were the loveliest and most sumptuous masquerades, with various liveries for the horses, with coursing of the bulls, with tilting, and with diverse music.[56]

The masking was probably the most important single feature. Molmenti notes the connection between this custom and the *commedia dell'arte:* "Carnival gradually came to be more and more thronged with masqueraders, the principal figures being the magnifico or pantaloon as he afterwards became, the *Zanni,* and the *Mattaccino.*"[57]

Saint Didier's comments, though late, are of interest. He notes, "The *Carnaval* of *Venice* is so Famous . . . that those of other Countries who are desirous to see *Venice,* wait this Opportunity." He attributes the popularity to ". . . the Custom of assuming any sort of Disguise, the great Liberty which all Masques every where enjoy." His very metaphors show the connection between Carnival and theater: "The Place of Saint *Mark* is the great Theater, upon which is to be seen the chief Appearance of the Carnaval" (Part 3, pp. 55–56).

Portia's disguise? This costume was worn by "Doctors of Laws from outside Venice, throughout Lombardy" ("Dottori di legge fuor di Venetia, per tutta la Lombardia"). We can easily imagine Portia dressed in such a robe and hat in Act 4, *The Merchant of Venice.* From Cesare Vecellio, *De gli habiti antichi, et moderni* (Venice, 1590), Sig. V5 verso. By permission of the British Library.

Another festival popular with foreigners was Ascension Day, shortened by the Venetians to "Sensa." Molmenti, writing about the period around 1600, claims that at this holiday over 100,000 people poured into Venice. When one recalls that the total population along about this time was probably 150,000–200,000, one can imagine the impact of the holiday on the city's consciousness, and on the consciousness of the visitors as well.

The chief feature of the Corpus Christi Day celebration was a solemn and magnificent procession through the Piazza di San Marco. Of particular interest to Jonson scholars is the following note, which relates to Celia's watching of the disguised Volpone performing in his "obscure nook of the piazza" (2.2. 34–39, 199 s.d.). Sansovino says, "And the women, placing themselves all around the piazza at the upper windows, awaited the rich pomp which was to come."[58] Richard Guylforde wrote in 1506 of the Corpus Christi procession that the ". . . forme and manner thereof excedyd all other that ever I sawe so moche that I can not wryte it" (p. 9).

A good example of the vividness with which the annual events of Venetian holiday celebration impressed visitors is Saint Didier's description of the Procession of the Holy sacrament: "Nothing can be more Glorious than *Venice* upon this Night, which is illuminated with Millions of Flambeaux, the Place of St. *Mark* being then one of the finest Sights imaginable. . ." (Part 1, p. 32).

In addition to annual events, the Venetians were famous all over Europe for their celebrations in honor of visits by foreign notables. By far the most well-known of these was what Volpone calls "the entertainment of the great Valois" (3.7.161). Henry III of France visited Venice in 1574, and Muir has found no fewer than fourteen extant pamphlets devoted only to this subject.[59] Details can wait until Chapter Five; here it is sufficient to note the importance of such celebrations in establishing the bright side of the European image of *Venezia-città-galante*.

In all the fine arts, too, Venice could offer much. The glitter of Venetian painting in the period is too well known to need description, but we should note that the music was outstanding also. Venetian madrigals, for instance, were regarded as particularly singable and hence suitable for domestic performance. Therefore many English composers in this form followed the Venetian school rather than Monteverdi.[60]

* * *

Every large European nation or linguistic group in the age of Shakespeare was reputed to have a characteristic vice; a well-known though fictional Danish prince, for instance, notes that "They clip us drunkards." Without any doubt the favorite vice to attribute to the Venetians was sexual licentiousness. As James Howell put it, "She is taxd all the World over for the latitud of liberty She gives to carnall pleasure, and the large conscience She hath under the navill" (p. 199 [Sig. Ee]). Many of the same writers who praise the splendors of Venice's legitimate pleasures also condemn *La Serenissima* for its illegitimate pleasures of a sexual kind. Saint Didier, for instance, asserts:

> Many of those who know *Rome* and *Venice*, are at a loss which of these two Cities is the most Libertine, and most plentifully serv'd with Courtisans. For my one part I am certain nothing can be equal to what is Practised at *Venice*. . . .(Part 3, p. 47)

Molementi goes so far as to blame moral decadence in general and courtesans in particular for the eventual fall of the Republic:

> The artistic temperament of the Italians threw a glamour of refinement and grace over vice itself; the aesthetic supplanted the moral judgment; the search for pleasure passed all limits, and voluptous living surely and steadily, day by day, sapped the energy of the brain and the vigour of the Arm.[61]

When Othello bitterly and sarcastically says to Desdemona, "I took you for that cunning whore of Venice" (4.2.89), his words would have struck a chord of recognition for practically every educated person in Western Europe. Venetian courtesans were indeed notorious; first of all, by their sheer number. Coryat's estimate of twenty thousand in 1608 is called "fantastic" by Molmenti, but the early sixteenth-century diarist Sanudo, himself a patriotic Venetian, puts the number at 11,654. Cavendish's servant Fox sets it at eight thousand in 1589.[62] Thus it seems likely that somewhere between five and ten per cent of the entire population was composed of prostitutes—a somewhat astounding proportion, by almost anyone's standards.

The courtesans were also famous for the openness with which they practiced their trade. Vecellio paints an interesting word picture of the "meretrici de' luoghi publici" at their windows and doorways. After describing their apparel, which featured bare breasts, he adds:

> But one cannot easily describe how they adorn their heads, how they come to the windows, frequenting even more the doorways and the street, to draw into the net the suckers that pass by. There they remain, singing amorous canzonets, but with little grace and conforming to their vile condition, making themselves heard by almost everybody by means of a raucous voice.[63]

That prostitutes were so numerous and their solicitations so open was possible only because the Venetian government tolerated—indeed, regulated—the trade. Courtesans were under the jurisdiction of the "Signiory of the Sanità," an agency named by Volpone (in a different context—2.2.144–45) that was a kind of Ministry of Health (*Delle cose notabili* 1587, Sig.I 7).

Coryat, with a religious fervor somewhat at odds with his minute and basically complimentary account of his meeting with the famous courtesan Margareta Aemiliana, denounces the official toleration of the trade: "A most ungodly thing without doubt that there should be a toleration of such licentious wantons in so glorious, so potent, so renowned a city" (I.402).

Several writers speculate about the reasons for this official toleration. Besides the idea already mentioned that it was a deliberate piece of statecraft designed to keep the lower classes in line, another idea is that the *Clarissimi* themselves enjoyed mistresses and were perhaps unwilling to legislate their own inconvenience. The Venetians claimed that they imported courtesans to preserve the honesty of local women. Saint Didier remarks sarcastically, ". . . the *Republick* seem'd to believe that the Sea-Air render'd this Disorder [i.e. lust] habitual and without remedy. . . ." The author of *Delle cose notablili* does indeed make the claim that Saint Didier is ridiculing.[64]

The Venetians were also accused of tolerating such huge numbers of whores because the whores were an important part of the famed "liberty" of Venice. Saint Didier comments, "This Famous Liberty draws Strangers hither in Multitudes, where the Pleasure and Diversions of the Place as sure empty their Pockets" (p. 46).

"This Famous Liberty" was a controversial subject. The Venetians and their admirers began with the definition of liberty as the freedom from foreign domination which Venice had for so long enjoyed and extended that definition in a questionable manner by asserting that in Venice an individual had "liberty," that is, freedom from arbitrary oppression.[65] I discuss the whole notion of Venetian liberty in connection with the dark side of its reputation as a *città-galante* because most writers, particularly the late seventeenth-century ones, argue that this famous liberty was really a euphemism for sexual licentiousness. As usual it is Saint Didier who has the most penetrating analysis. He asserts that this liberty "which is at *Venice* so much in every one's Mouth, even from the meanest of the People to the first of the Senators" consists mainly in indulging in pleasures and being disrespectful to one's betters: ". . . it seems to me that this Liberty of *Venice* is properly a Political Libertinism" (Part 3, pp. 42–43). He adds:

> The Liberty of *Venice* makes every thing Authentick, for whatsoever the Life is, or Religion one Professes, provided, you do not Talk, or Attempt any thing against the State, or the Nobility, one may be sure to Live unmolested, for no Body will go about to Censure their Conduct, or to oppose the Disorders of their Neighbors. (Part 3, pp. 44–45)

A vicious circle developed: the City's reputation for not having much of a conscience from the girdle downward and for not looking into anyone else's sexual habits attracted rich, licentious foreigners; and the more those foreigners flocked in, the more (doubtless) Venice really did become a city of sexual license. Such foreigners were attracted to Venice as early as 1565, and this aspect of the city's reputation continued to grow.[66]

Unfortunately for Venice's respectable women, the city's reputation for sexual license rubbed off, to some extent, on them. The Milanese writer, Ortensio Landi (or Lando), says Venetian women ". . . are beautiful in form, but to speak plainly they have the gestures and mores of whores."[67] They did not help matters when they adopted—doubtless with the tacit consent of their husbands, be it noted—a peculiar public fashion in clothing: bare, or nearly bare, breasts in public, on which cosmetics were worn. Moryson says that the breasts are partially concealed by lace and white makeup:

> The women of Venice weare gownes, leaving all the necke and brest bare, and they are closed before with a lace, so open, as a man may see the linnen which they lap about their bodies, to make them seeme fat, the Italians most loving fat women. They shew their naked necks and breasts, and likewise their dugges, bound up and swelling with linnen, and all made white by art. (1907 ed., IV.220)

Henri Estienne speaks (in 1578) of this fashion as astonishing and unfamiliar (at least to Frenchmen). Even his word for it, "espoitrinement," is clearly a novelty.[68] In the 1590s Villamont says specifically that the fashion is not to be found in Venice's neighboring cities: "But the Romans, Milanese, Neapolitans, Florentines, Ferrarese, and other dames of Italy are much more modest in this regard, for . . . they do not uncover their breasts."[69] Coryat objects to the fashion on moral grounds: "For I beleeve unto many that have prurientem libidem, they would minister a great incentive and fomentation of luxurious desires" (I.399–400).

Exposing the breasts was only the most spectacular of many colorful fashions adopted by Venetian women. Among these were the platform shoes called chopins (which Hamlet mentions in talking to the players), and the customs of bleaching the hair and wearing heavy cosmetics and splendid clothing. Moryson notes: "For this attire the women of Venice are proverbially said to be, Grande de legni, Grosse di straci, rosse di bettito, bianche di calcina: that is tall with wood, fat with ragges, red with painting, and white with chalke." (IV. 220)

I would not argue that Venice's function as a fashion center for Europe necessarily had anything to do with its reputation for sexual immorality any more that Paris's similar reputation (say, in the 1920s) contributed to that city's fame as a fleshpot. But the two kinds of reputations do seem to go together, so perhaps there *is* a connection at some obscure level.

Whether as a result of their tastes in fashions or because of guilt by association attributable to the fame of Venetian courtesans, Venetian wives had some reputation (Iago exaggerates it) for straying from their husbands when they could. But such straying, according to writer after writer, was almost impossible because of the extreme jealousy of Venetian husbands. Amelot de la Houssaye places the chief blame on the men, asserting that they care far more for their courtesans than for their wives: ". . . their Mistresses are much more chargeable to them than their Wives, whom they use as their Servants." He adds:

> But how indifferent soever they are for their Wives, they are so jealous of them, that in Carneval-time they dog them wherever they go; some have gone so far as to stab them upon bare suspition, and have been thought brave Gentlemen for their pains. . . [Cf. *Othello*]. But they may well be jealous, for as wise as they are, there

> will be stealing into their Quarters, and the *Senat* must keep Guards upon their Ladies . . . unless they can be contented with a Contreband Nobility. (pp. 275–76)

The traveler John Ray makes a typical comment: "Women of any Fashion are kept in great restraint here, seldom appearing abroad, except it be at Church, when they are sure to have an old Woman for their Guardian."[70]

Saint Didier tells a fine anecdote on this subject. Chopins having just gone *out* of fashion, a foreign visitor commented to a Venetian magnifico that shoes with lower heels are after all "more Commodious," to which "one of the Councellors replied with an Austere Meen, and twice repeated it, They are indeed too Commodious, *Pur tròpo Commodi, pur tròpi*" (Part 3, pp. 23–24).

Because of the restraints on their movements, wives were sometimes said to be able to slip away only with the aid of their masks at Carnival time. Such ladies "as have Intrigues do at this time by a Thousand different ways deceive both Husband and Guards," Carnival being the season in which "the Gallants get in the Harvest of their Amours" (Saint Didier, Part 3, pp. 56–57).

Pierre d'Avity provides a good summary of the dark side of *Venezia-città-galante* from the point of view of one who admires Venice but laments her immorality. The Venetian Republic, he says, looks as if it will last forever:

> . . . and although it seemes to some that for the great wickednesse which is committed dayly within the citie of Venice, she cannot long avoid her totall ruine and subversion, yet others know that besides the magistrat who doth his best endeavour to reforme all disorders, there are many devout persons whose prayers would stay this desolation. (Sig. Zzv, p. 530)

* * *

Which, then, of the two sides of the Myth of Venice, the bright or the dark, was predominant in the age of Shakespeare and Jonson? This is difficult to say, although despite what one historian calls the "almost obsessive preoccupation of foreigners with the licentiousness of Venice,"[71] I suspect that, all in all, the bright side was the dominant one. But the question is not of great importance here, since both sides are exciting and colorful and thus of great interest to the dramatist.

Stoye summarizes clearly and wittily the reactions of Englishmen to Italy in general, and his remarks fit Venice as well:

> It is difficult to say . . . whether the Elizabethans and Jacobeans harped more constantly on the attractions or the repulsiveness with which they credited the Italian world; and for a few there was also the attraction of repulsiveness. A violent fluctuation from one extreme to another, when Italy appeared before the mind's eye, is one of the most familiar characteristics of their great dramatists. (p. 109)

V. The Myth of Venice in England

The attractions and repulsions (and the attraction of the repulsions) of Venice in England were much the same as in other parts of Europe, which is why in the foregoing discussion I have freely mingled English sources with those from other places. But two additional points need to be made: (1) Venice was sometimes thought of in England as different from other parts of Italy, and when that happened, generally (2) Venice was thought of more favorably than those other parts.

To get some distance toward understanding Venice's favored status in England, one can compare Lewkenor's *History and Commonwealth of Venice* (1599) with Sir Robert Dallington's *A Survey of the Great Dukes State of Tuscany in . . . 1596* (1605). Lewkenor has been accused of hyperbole in praising Venice,[72] and this charge is certainly true. But, as I have argued elsewhere, his hyperbole is really typical of, not more effusive than, that of most European observers who looked mainly on Venice's bright side.[73] Even people from distant parts of the earth, says Lewkenor, all ". . . speake of the cittie of *Venice* . . . to the highest of all admiration, as being a thing of the greatest worthinesse, and most infinitely remarkable, that they had seen in the whole course of their travels" (Preface, Sig. Av-A2). Dallington, by contrast, dwells so strongly on the dark side of the Elizabethan image of Italy that the Grand Duke's representative in England asked that the book be suppressed.[74]

The differences between Lewkenor's Venice and Dallington's Tuscany may, of course, result from factors other than Venice's favored status; they could, for instance, be due largely to differences in the outlook and values of the two men. Therefore an even better test is provided by two books written half a century later—better because they were written by the same author. In his *Instructions for Foreign Travel* (1642), James Howell balances the light and dark sides of Italy as a whole:

> The *Italian*, being the *greatest embracer of pleasures*, the *greatest Courtier of Ladies* of any other. Here he [the young traveler] shall find Vertue and Vice, Love and Hatred, Atheisme and Religion in their extremes; being a witty contemplative people; and *Corruptio optimi est pessima. Of the best wines you make your tartest vinegar.*[75]

But nine years later, in *A Survey of the Signorie of Venice*, he dwells on the glories of *La Serenissima*, as, for example, in the poem (quoted earlier) about Venice and Venus *(S.PQ.V.)*. He tries to put the vices of the place in the best light possible. For instance, he admits that there are a lot of courtesans, but, he adds, She (the Republic) ". . . suffers not those frayl vessels of plesure to mingle with her other Daughters in Church-Communion." He also admits that Venetians are given to sexual pleasure, but adds that ". . . *Naples* exceed[s] Her in this kind." Nor is Venice entirely to blame for the prevalence of sexual vice: ". . . She may receave this infection from the *Greek* and the *Turk* Her Neighbors." Finally on this subject he adds:

> . . . they say ther be multitudes of reclusd men and women in *Venice*, who by their austere cours of continency make som compensation for this loosnes in others, and keep Her Citty from *sinking*; for when the last cense was made, ther were neer upon 5000 Fryers and Nunns. . . . (pp. 8, 199[Sig. Ee])

William Lithgow, in a riot of alliteration, praises ". . . the glorie of Gallants, Galleries, Gallies, Galleasses, and Gallouns," but cuts his description short: "Wherefore since the scituation thereof, and the decorements of their beautifull Palaces, are so well knowne by the better sort, I desist. . . ."[76] This last comment clearly indicates that Lithgow thought the English market for description of Venice to be saturated.

Venice, then, was the favored Italian city. Others were thought to be over the hill: "Venice alone remained comparatively pure amid degradation and servility elsewhere."[77] This comment, with its political flavor, suggests that the principal reasons for Venice's favored status were probably political ones. To begin with, England and the Venetians had similar geopolitical interests about 1600: they were both interested in curbing Hapsburg power in the Mediterranean. James was even more eager than Elizabeth had been for friendly relations with Venice, and the regularizing of diplomatic ties in 1604 must have added to the tendency of Englishmen to think more highly of Venice than of other Italian states.

And, as James's first Ambassador to Venice observed in a letter of 23 May 1603, Venice is ". . . a Signory that with long neutrality of State is at length (as it seemeth) almost slipped into a neutrality of religion."[78] Even the suspicion that Venice was basically anti-Papal would have raised *La Serenissima* in the eyes of many Englishmen. And that suspicion had long existed; since 1173, Molmenti notes, Venice had been under papal interdict five times, culminating (though too late to have affected the three plays under close scrutiny in this book) in the troubles of 1606–1607 in which Paolo Sarpi was, from the English point of view, the hero. Indeed, Sarpi created such a stir that Cecil and King James tried to persuade him to visit England.[79]

Finally, Venice was the preferred Italian city partly by default—the alternatives being less palatable from a religious and/or political point of view. After all, Rome was the seat of the Pope, Naples was long associated with Spanish power, and Florence was the home of Machiavelli. The patriotic Englishman really had little choice.

And so the stage was set for the favorable growth of the Myth in England, and grow it did—so vigorously that it furnished considerable source material for three of the greatest plays of the age. To those plays we now turn.

3
The Merchant of Venice and the Myth

Antonio. The Duke cannot deny the course of law;
For the commodity that strangers have
With us in Venice, if it be denied,
Will much impeach the justice of the state,
Since that the trade and profit of the city
Consisteth of all nations.

(3.3.26–31)

There are three aspects of Venetian social and economic history in the sixteenth century, all connected with the Myth, which are of special interest to students of *The Merchant of Venice.* One is the idea, already sketched, that Venice was declining as an economic and military power. The second is a related phenomenon which modern historians call the turn landward. The third is the notion, clearly related to the Myth of the impartiality of Venetian justice, that the Jewish community in Venice was especially rich and numerous and that Venice treated Jews especially well. The first bears upon our interpretation of the character of Antonio; the second, upon both Bassanio and Portia; the third, upon Shylock.[1]

I. Antonio and the Decline of Venice

When we look not directly at Antonio himself, but at the atmosphere of mercantile wealth that surrounds him at the beginning of the play, we are seeing against a background provided by the bright side of the Myth of Venice. References to Antonio's connections with those trading activities that had made Venice great are particularly frequent in the early scenes. The first mention of his "argosies with portly sail" (1.1.9) probably made some in Shakespeare's audience think of Venice's mercantile splendor. The *Oxford English Dictionary* (OED) tells us that "argosy" is derived from Ragusa (the modern Dubrovnik, in Yugoslavia), a Venetian possession in the sixteenth century. Hence, says the OED, the historical and poetic meaning "a merchant-vessel of the largest size and burden; esp. those of Ragusa and Venice."

Antonio's wealth is being connected imaginatively here with trade in vast ships. Salerio is very accurate, as I mentioned earlier, in referring to Antonio's typical cargo as spices and silks—the two commodities that had historically been the source of most Venetian profits (1.1.33, 34). While Shakespeare may be drawing here on Marlowe's *Jew of Malta*—Barabas's argosy from Alexandria carries the very same cargo—this may also be a piece of accurate Venetian local color.[2] Whatever the source, the reference to these commodities impressively connotes the Myth of "Venetia la Ricca."

The far-flung destinations given for Antonio's ships also suggest the vast wealth of the Venetian merchant empire. Shylock notes, ". . . he hath an argosy bound to Tripolis, another to the Indies; . . . he hath a third at Mexico, a fourth for England, and other ventures he hath, squand'red abroad" (1.3.18–21). Salerio twice mentions the wreck of the one that had been bound for England (2.8.28–30, 3.1.2–4), and Tubal mentions Antonio's "argosy cast away, coming from Tripolis" (3.1.100–01)—all consistent with Shylock's initial list. Bassanio, too, gives a list; this one fuller (presumably making specific the "other ventures"): "From Tripolis, from Mexico, and England, / From Lisbon, Barbary, and India" (3.2.268–69). The Indies/India discrepancy may be due to a textual problem, but it seems to me likely that Shakespeare did not bother to make the two lists identical because he was more interested in the splendor suggested by these destinations that he was in either rigid consistency or minute adherence to historical fact. For the truth is that neither Shylock's nor Bassanio's list is notable for such minute adherence. Tripolis (probably the one near present-day Beirut, not the one in North Africa) was indeed a major port for Venetian shipping, and there was a fair amount of trade between England and Venice (although, increasingly, in English rather than Venetian bottoms).[3] Lisbon and Barbary, too, were plausible Venetian destinations. Venice's giant argosies did not ply the Atlantic or the Indian Ocean, so that Mexico, India, and the East *or* West Indies are, from a literal point of view, inaccurate. But the lists certainly make the point about the magnificence of Venetian merchant shipping.

The same point is perhaps made by the epithet "royal merchant." Gratiano asks, "How doth that royal merchant, good Antonio?" (3.2.239); and in the trial scene the Duke laments that Antonio has been subjected to misfortunes "Enow to press a royal merchant down"(4.1.29). Shakespeare may simply be referring to the English custom of royal charters for merchant companies; but he may instead (or also) be referring to the splendor displayed by leading Venetians, many of whom were merchants. William Thomas, for instance, comments:

> For he that will row through the Canale Grande and mark well the fronts of the houses on both sides shall see them more like the doings of princes than private men. And I have been with good reason persuaded that in Venice be above 200 palaces able to lodge any king. (p. 65)

Are we to think of Antonio as inhabiting one of these two hundred "royal" palaces?

But when we turn from Antonio's appurtenances to Antonio himself, the picture is quite different. All of the references to his wealth are placed in a context of his melancholy and his losses. Indeed, the very first speech of the play is of his sadness, not his argosies. The more one examines his character in the context of the Venetian Myth, the more one sees the darker tones. I believe that we will understand his character better if we see it primarily in the context of the *decline* of Venetian power and wealth.

Of the causes usually alleged in the sixteenth century for the reputed decline, the one most relevant to Antonio is the idea that the Portuguese discovery and exploitation of the sea route around Africa severely damaged the Venetian spice trade. The idea was available in English, and early enough for *Merchant.* Fenton's translation of Guicciardini (1579) states it emphatically:

> . . . the king of *Portugall* . . . had taken from them [the Venetians] and appropriated to him selfe, the traffike of spices, which the Marchantes and shippes bringing out of *Alexandria* . . . to *Venice,* they sent dispersed with a wonderfull profite through all the provinces in Chrystendome. The which alteration beeing a thing of the most merite and memorie of all others that have hapned in the worlde

since many ages, and, for the harmes which the Citie of *Venice* receyved by it . . . it can not much alter the estate of our historie to speake somewhat of it at large.[4]

The idea of Venice in decline is good to keep in the back of one's mind when Antonio's melancholy is discussed. I certainly do not mean to construct an historical allegory here in which Antonio somehow stands for the entire Venetian merchant trade, and its decline is symbolized by his sadness. That would be reductive. But the general idea of the decline may well have made more plausible the bankruptcy of the merchant whom Shakespeare found in his source.[5]

Antonio is, I think, in financial difficulty even before the news comes concerning the wreck of his argosy on Goodwin Sands. He puts on a brave front in talking with his casual acquaintances, but tells Bassanio a somewhat different story. To be specific, he first denies to Salerio and Solanio that money problems lie at the root of his melancholy: "Believe me, no. I thank my fortune for it, / My ventures are not in one bottom trusted, / Nor to one place" (1.1.41–43). So far, so good. The rest of the play corroborates these claims. But Antonio goes further: ". . . nor is my whole estate / Upon the fortune of this present year" (1.1.43–44). I take this to mean that even if every one of his current ventures were to fail, he would still have money in reserve. We may grant that the odds against every one of his ships failing to come home were astronomical, but the fact remains that, like another "merchant" in a different era, Willy Loman, Antonio is inclined to exaggerate his financial resources when facing the world at large. To his intimate friend, Bassanio, by contrast, Antonio frankly admits, "Thou know'st that all my fortunes are at sea" (1.1.177). Antonio is not simply exaggerating to Bassanio in order to make his sacrifice seem greater, for events in the play prove that all his fortunes *were,* in fact, at sea. Even Shylock, an outsider (though a man who keeps up eagerly with the latest business news on the Rialto), is aware that Antonio's "means are in supposition" (1.3.17).

There is a connection, I believe, between Antonio's exaggeration to his two acquaintances and his melancholy. Despite the strong argument of Lawrence Danson to the contrary, I suggest that Salerio and Solanio have, unlike Rosencrantz and Guildenstern, plucked out the heart of Antonio's mystery. They first attribute the sadness to his financial affairs (1.1.8–40); when Antonio rejects this idea, Solanio suggests that the melancholy is because of love (1.1.46). Antonio indignantly rejects this notion also ("Fie, fie!"), but we do not have to believe his protestations. I think that Salerio and Solanio are correct in both their guesses.[6] I am not so taken with the economic explanation that I cannot see the virtues of the emotional one—the timing for the latter being right, Antonio having just lately "marvellously chang'd" (1.1.76) and also just lately discovered that his beloved Bassanio is planning a pilgrimage to some lady (1.1.119–21). Antonio knows the potential that wedding bells have for breaking up the old gang. But the two explanations (love and money) are not mutually exclusive.

I believe that the play is more poignant, more powerful, if we accept the two explanations than if we leave the mystery intact, for even the economic explanation has powerful emotional overtones. Portia reasons that Antonio and Bassanio have spent so much time together that they must needs have grown to resemble each other closely (3.4.11–18). She may be right: it may be that while Bassanio was "something showing a more swelling port / Than my faint means would grant continuance" (1.1.124–25), Antonio was doing much the same—except that instead of spending money excessively, he was busy convincing the world that he had more than he actually did. Both men are guilty of having fished for that gudgeon, opinion. Keeping up a hypocritical front can be a heavy weight on the emotions of a sensitive soul like Antonio.

That Salerio and Solanio are correct in their guesses is not at all inconsistent with the Antonio that we see in the latter half of the play. The muted death wish in his "embraced heaviness" (2.8.52) and in "I am a tainted wether of the flock" (4.1.114) is understandable in one who, at that moment, believes that he has failed in his role as Venetian merchant and failed , as the marriage of Bassanio indicates, to hold first place in Bassanio's heart. I cannot agree with Solanio that Antonio loves the world only for the sake of Bassanio (2.8.50). Antonio also cares about wealth—not for its own sake, like a miser, but for the status it confers. When given the chance to utter what everyone except, perhaps, Portia supposes will be his last words, one of his main topics is the miseries of poverty:

> For herein Fortune shows herself more kind
> Than is her custom. It is still her use
> To let the wretched man outlive his wealth,
> To view with hollow eye and wrinkled brow

An age of poverty; from which ling'ring penance
Of such misery doth she cut me off. (4.1.267–72)

After Portia turns the tables on Shylock, Antonio shows some mercy to the Jew; but it is noteworthy that he has (by means of whatever portions of Shylock's money he is to keep or administer) once again become a man of substance. The knowledge that he is once again solvent is also, perhaps, what enables him to accompany Bassanio to Belmont, the seat of his rival. It is as if he does not have to have love *and* money; he can subsist on either. But he cannot do without both.

In the end, of course, he has not only some portion of Shylock's wealth but also the wealth from three of his argosies "richly come to harbor suddenly" (5.1.277). His reply to this news, "I am dumb," may betoken amazement and gratitude that Fate has restored him fully to one of his two roles: he can once again be The Merchant of Venice.

II. The Venetian Turn Landward and *The Merchant of Venice*

Clearly related to the idea of Venice as a declining power is the idea that modern historians have called the turn landward. Because of the successes of the Turks and Portuguese, trade doubtless began to seem less attractive to Venetian aristocrats; and the increase of Venetian dominions in northeastern Italy made landowning more attractive to the wealthier nobles. Even in Shakespeare's day the wisdom of the turn landward was considered debatable.[7] Whether harmful to the Republic or not, mainland villas proliferated during the sixteenth century. Most patricians had at least one; many had several. Coryat writes, "When I passed downe the River to Venice I saw many goodly faire houses and Palaces of pleasure on both sides of the River Brenta, which belong to the Gentlemen of Venice" (I.300).

It is not surprising that accompanying this trend we find a trend toward according merchants a lower social status than landowning aristocrats. While such a ranking had long prevailed in other European nations, it was a relatively new phenomenon in Venice. Indeed, the change in Venetian attitudes may result from economic trends as well as from social pressures generated by the attitudes of other nations.

The changing attitudes of Venetians are apparent in such works as Giovanni Maria Memmo's dialogue on the formation of a perfect citizen, soldier, and merchant (Venice, 1563). He gives lip service to the mercantile foundations of Venice, but only reluctantly. He argues that through the ages merchants in various empires have not been of the governing class because they have had their own pockets as their primary goal rather than the good of the state. However, he adds politicly: "although in the Venetian Republic merchants have always governed and administered public affairs with great prudence."[8] No such ambivalence is in Girolamo Muzio's *Il gentilhuomo* (Venice, 1571). He declares roundly that to be a merchant is to lose one's nobility.[9]

How much Shakespeare knew of the turn landward is hard to guess; but in view of the many kinds of sources available to him (see Chapter 1), surely we are justified in asking what consequences would follow in our interpretation of the play if we assume that he was familiar with the idea.

Portia and Bassanio are clearly portrayed as aristocrats. In the well-known line "In Belmont is a lady richly left" (1.1.161) critics usually concentrate on the words "richly left" because of the debate about Bassanio's mercenary motives. But the word "lady" may be just as significant; her social rank is indicated even before her financial status. Portia is a lady of leisure. She has seemingly unlimited funds; yet, as critics with Marxist leanings have commented, there is no mention at Belmont of such vulgar subjects as work.[10] Like all aristocrats, she has presumably inherited her wealth, and—perhaps just as important—the ancestral seat. With Belmont, we assume, comes land and lots of it. Despite certain hints of trouble in this paradise, it seems on the whole rather like Penshurst as Jonson imagined that "ancient pile."

If the first mention of Portia identifies her as a lady, the first mention at Belmont of Bassanio's name identifies him as "a scholar and a soldier, that came hither in company of the Marquis of Montferrat" (1.2.113–14). Scholars were not necessarily aristocratic, although many were—especially in Italy. William Thomas praises Italian universities because they consist ". . . not of such students alone as most commonly are brought up in our universities (mean men's children set to school in hope to live upon hired learning), but for the more part of noblemen's sons and of the best gentlemen, that study more for knowledge and pleasure than for curiosity or lucre" (p. 10). By way of evidence, Thomas adds, "For lightly there passeth no Shrovetide without running at the tilt, tourneying, fighting at the barriers, and otherlike feats of arms, handled and furnished after the best sort; the greatest doers whereof are scholars" (pp. 10–11). Finally Thomas comments specifically on the university dominated by Venice: "This last winter, lying in Padua, with diligent search I learned that the number of scholars there was little less than fifteen hundred; wherof I dare say a thousand at the least were gentlemen" (p.11).

Soldiers, like scholars, were not necessarily gentlemen, but often were. No wonder Thomas speaks of scholars, soldiers, and gentlemen in almost the same breath; there was clearly a presumption in the Veneto that one might well be all three. We note too that Bassanio first came to Belmont in the company of a marquis, a rank familiar to English audiences.

Furthermore there is something quintessentially aristocratic about Bassanio's prodigality. We know today, although Shakespeare may not have, that Venice was full of such impoverished patricians. Power and wealth were falling increasingly into the hands of just a few families, leaving the other families in the Golden Book with just as many rights and privileges theoretically, but little power in *realpolitik* terms:

> Venetian commerce and industry, which had survived the shock of the opening of the Atlantic, faltered at last, destroying the financial security of a considerable section of the aristocracy. Foreign commerce had been the area of preferred activity for the less wealthy nobles who now saw this avenue of prosperity close. Only those nobles with considerable capital reserves were able to invest in agriculture and reap the profits available from the exploitation of the terra firma, the mainland possessions of the Republic. Thus while one section of the nobility was sinking into poverty, a small element was becoming immensely rich.[11]

In the context of Venetian history, then, Portia may be seen as a landed aristocrat of the Terra Firma and Bassanio as an impoverished but genteel scholar and soldier of the lower Venetian aristocracy; we may even imagine that his father or grandfather had been a merchant. But now he must marry money to survive. If we see Portia and Bassanio from this perspective, how does this affect our perception of the play as a whole?

The play seems less a fairy tale or conventional New Comedy and more a story of the contemporary world. The contemporary features in the characterization of Portia and Bassanio seem particularly striking when one contrasts the play with the story in

Il pecorone. In the novella (which is after all a product of the fourteenth century), the lady is aristocratic, all right, but has sinister overtones of a *belle dame sans merci.* She lures lovers into a kind of wager: if they can possess her sexually, she will marry them; if not, she gets to keep all of their money and possessions. The Bassanio figure, named Giannetto, fails twice to perform sexually (because he was drugged), then finally succeeds. The unnamed lady is not a whit repentant about her earlier predatory behavior, though she does marry the hero as promised.

Portia, by contrast, has retained the desirability and near-perfection of fairy tale heroines, but at the same time is anchored in the realities of sixteenth-century history. It is true that she is only to be won by the fairy-tale casket test; but Belmont is so clearly located in geography that one turn-of-the-century scholar, Theodore Elze, claimed to have it pinpointed.[12]

Bassanio, too, is a far cry from the spoiled brat of *Il pecorone.* Like Portia, he too becomes a more realistic figure if seen as a representative of a social group (the lower aristocracy) which has perhaps been deprived of its traditional way of making a living, its members not yet quite comfortable with the roles of scholar and soldier. Bassanio's solution to what he should do with his life has been, until he meets Portia, to spend the remains of his (meager?) patrimony on high living and hospitality. Even on borrowed money, he hires Launcelot, a "huge feeder," and holds feasts (2.2.171–72, II.v.46). Like Petruchio, he is a recognizable social type who (before falling in love) has one overriding motive: he comes to wive it wealthily in Belmont; if wealthily, then happily in Belmont.

Besides nudging the play away from the past and toward the present, seeing Bassanio and Antonio in the context of changing Venetian (and long-standing English) attitudes toward the status of merchants has another major effect: it can help us to understand the subtle sense of strain between the two.

For there is, I think, such a sense of strain. Bassanio is reluctant in the first scene to tell Antonio about the lady and about his request for more money. Doubtless his reluctance results mainly from embarrassment; he knows that Antonio's love is so intense that his friend might secretly resent the prospect of his marriage. Bassanio may also be embarrassed at borrowing more from someone he already owes. But if we assume a small but still nagging gap in social rank between the two, we find the scene enriched. Bassanio is borrowing from, and proposing to desert, his social inferior. At the beginning of their private interview, Bassanio talks of Gratiano as long as he can, but Antonio—impatient—wants to get right to the heart of the matter: "Well, tell me now what lady is the same / To whom you swore a secret pilgrimage, / That you to-day promis'd to tell me of?" (1.1.119-21). Bassanio attempts to hide his embarrassment through rhetoric, as many scholars before and after him have: he resorts to the elaborate and ingenious analogy about the arrows. Again, Antonio has no patience with these flowers of rhetoric: "You know me well, and herein spend but time / To wind about my love with circumstance" (153–54). We are dealing here not with two men from the same social class who just happen to differ in temperament, but instead with two men whose education and standing in society, though not vastly different, are yet different enough to create problems.

Bassanio is present during the scene in which Shylock and Antonio come to agreement, but there is surprisingly litttle verbal interchange between the two friends. The parting of the two in the second act was obviously quite tender; but there may be significance in the fact that it is described to us by Salerio and Solanio, not dramatized. Unlike Giannetto in the source, Bassanio is not guilty of forgetting the bond because of the happiness of the marriage; but his desire to go immediately to Antonio's aid may result not only from love but also from a bit of noblesse oblige.

The sense of strain that I am positing works both ways. I find in Antonio's letter to Bassanio, for instance, more than praiseworthy self-abnegation between equals; the tone is that of a social inferior addressing a superior. In contrast to the rest of the scene, the letter is all in prose (often the language of hard-handed men in Shakespeare); and he tells Bassanio his troubles in a straightforward way that is quite unlike the arrow analogy: "Sweet Bassanio, my ships have all miscarried, my creditors grow cruel, my estate is very low, my bond to the Jew is forfeit; and since in paying it, it is impossible I should live, all debts are clear'd between you and I, if I might but see you at my death" (3.2.315–20). The next sentence is almost astounding in its diffidence: "Notwithstanding, use your pleasure; if your love do not persuade you to come, let not my letter" (320–22).

Even the courtroom scene may show strain between the two. When Antonio asks Bassanio to quit pleading with Shylock, the main theme of the speech is Shylock's heartlessness; but it has echoes of his earlier impatience with Bassanio as well: "Therefore I do beseech you / Make no moe offers, use no farther means,

/ But with all brief and plain conveniency / Let me have judgment and the Jew his will" (4.1.80–83). Does not this statement have a tone quite similar to "You know me well, and herein spend but time / To wind about my love with circumstance"? Finally, in this scene, Antonio has to ask Bassanio to give away the ring, a request which would have cost him more pain if they were not quite social equals than if they were.

Antonio is not really at home in Belmont; Portia treats him with cordiality but also, I think, formality, while Bassanio talks to him hardly at all. The superiority of this aristocratic pair to Antonio is perhaps symbolized by Antonio's learning of the safe arrival of his three argosies, not through his own news network, but through the rather mysterious medium of Portia: "You shall not know by what strange accident / I chanced on this letter" (5.1.278–79) is at one level simply a convenience enabling Shakespeare to wind up the play without tedious explanations, but it may at another reflect Portia's superiority to Antonio.[13]

I do not mean to imply that there is not a genuine and powerful love between Antonio and Bassanio. People then, as now, quite commonly loved each other across social boundaries. But boundaries do increase the possibilities for misunderstandings and minor irritations, and this pair has many. If I am right in attributing some of the sense of strain to slight inequality in social rank, the result is to make Antonio's part, already, as he says, "a sad one," more poignant still.

III. Shylock and the Jews of Venice

The character Shylock clearly has mythical dimensions. If, as Granville-Barker does, we compare the play with "Jack and the Beanstalk," then Shylock must be the Giant.[14] In early allegorizations of the flesh-bond story, the creditor is seen as the Devil; and Leslie Fiedler compares him (in Freudian terms) to an ogre.[15] This originally quasi-mythical character is anchored in credible, if not quite realistic, historical detail.

Shylock is in need of anchoring in ways in which Antonio, say, is not. While Shakespeare, in creating Antonio, was able to use both the glitter of the Venetian mercantile world and (I have argued) the sense of sadness at its decline, London had lots of wealthy merchants; many in Shakespeare's audience would have unconsciously compared Antonio with them.[16] But the audience had little or no experience with actual Jews; here, then, the Venetian setting was especially useful because the English knew that there *were* rich Jews in Venice who were allowed to practice their religion openly. Nearly all English travelers mention the Jewish community in Venice probably because, to them, it was so unusual.[17] Jews had been officially expelled from England in 1290, and those who were in Shakespeare's London had to practice their faith secretly. There were not very many of these crypto-Jews; the number has been estimated at between eighty and ninety.[18] Venice, by contrast, was credited in 1587 with 1,157, a figure which Lewkenor repeats.[19] Coryat's estimate (I.370) of between five and six thousand is surely far too high, but it underscores that the numbers were by no means inconsiderable.

One of the reasons for the number of Jews in Venice was that the *Ebrei* were said to be treated better there than in most other parts of Europe. In 1581 Sansovino states:

> These Jews, through the business of lending money, are very rich, and would rather live in Venice than in other parts of Italy because violence and tyranny are not used on them as elsewhere, and they are secure in their every need concerning their wealth. . . .Because they repose in a singular peace, they enjoy this country as if it were the Promised Land.[20]

Modern historians confirm much of what Sansovino says, minus (of course) his hyperbole. Roth, for instance, writing from a strongly pro-Jewish point of view, argues that the Jews in Venice were not subjected to nearly so much religious persecution as in other parts of Italy.[21]

The wealth of the Venetian Jews had been noted in English by Thomas:

> It is almost incredible what gain the Venetians receive by the usury of the Jews, both privately and in common. For in every city the Jews keep open shops of usury, taking gages of ordinary for fifteen in the hundred by the year, and if at the year's end the gage be not redeemed it is forfeit, or at the least done away to a great disadvantage, by reason whereof the Jews are out of measure wealthy in those parts. (Thomas, p. 69)

The most important way in which the Venetian setting renders Shylock more credible lies in the powerful idea—one of the main components of the Myth of Venice—that all nations, including Jews, could get justice from *La Serenissima.* Sansovino cites this perception as one of the main reasons why Jews preferred Venice:

"They attain justice against anyone, whoever he might be."[22] This facet of the Myth was already known to Ser Giovanni in 1378, although he is vague on the point: ". . . but as Venice was a place where justice was strictly administered, and the Jew had his pretensions grounded on publick and received forms, nobody dared to oppose him. . ." (*Shakespeare's Library,* I. 343–44).

It is difficult to believe that Shakespeare knew of the reputation of Venetian justice only from that bare mention in his source, for there are no fewer than three passages in *Merchant* in which the point is made in a more complex and elaborate fashion than it is in *Il pecorone.* First, Salerio reports that Shylock "plies the Duke at morning and at night, / And doth impeach the freedom of the state, / If they deny him justice" (3.2.277–79). Antonio himself, in a passage which is also the epigraph for this chapter, gives the fullest exposition of the principle:

> The Duke cannot deny the course of law;
> For the commodity that strangers have
> With us in Venice, if it be denied,
> Will much impeach the justice of the state,
> Since that the trade and profit of the city
> Consisteth of all nations. (3.3.26–31)

Antonio, true to the mercantile ideology in which he has been reared, well knows why even Jews must be given justice: "the trade and profit of the city." Finally Shylock himself dwells on the idea at the outset of the trial scene:

> And by our holy Sabaoth have I sworn
> To have the due and forfeit of my bond.
> If you deny it, let the danger light
> Upon your charter and your city's freedom! (4.1.36–39)

That the text so insists upon the supposed impartiality of Venetian law shows how useful this aspect of the Myth was in rendering the whole fantastic pound-of-flesh story more credible. One might go so far as to say that the myth of Venice the Just is almost as important to the play as the myth of Venice the Rich.

But beneath the myth of fair treatment (to which even some of the Jews themselves subscribed—or pretended to)[23] there was as always a dark and shameful discrimination against Jews, both in historical Venice and in the Venice of the play. Probably Shakespeare did not know much about the precise forms that the actual discrimination took, since few accurate details show up in the play. Historically the discrimination took three main forms: mode of dress, place of residence, and economic restrictions.

The mode of dress which branded one a Jew changed through the centuries. In the fourteenth century, Sansovino says, the Jews were forced to wear on their breast the letter or figure "o" of the size of a loaf of bread, and in the fifteenth to wear the same symbol hung from the neck by a yellow cord (Sansovino 1581, Sig. Mm). Many accounts, both Italian and English, describe the discriminatory mark of Shakespeare's day as a beret; but they disagree as to whether it was red or yellow: Sansovino says yellow, but the traveler, Laurence Aldersey, says red.[24]

Against this background it is interesting to place Shylock's "Jewish gaberdine" (1.3.112). No one has yet been able to connect this allusion with historical fact, or to explain it satifactorily in any other manner.[25] Nor can I. But two sources in English—one published early enough for Shakespeare to have read—describe a kind of garment worn only during religious services in the synagogue. Aldersey (1589) describes it as follows: ". . . as for their apparell, all of them weare a large white lawne over their garment, which reacheth from their head, downe to the ground" (Sig. P7). Coryat (1611) is obviously describing the same garment, but the details vary widely: ". . . every one of them whatsoever he be, man or childe, weareth a kind of light yellowish vaile, made of Linsie Woolsie (as I take it) over his shoulders, something worse then our courser Holland, which reacheth a little beneath the middle of their backes" (I.372). I do not see how this garment can have suggested "gaberdine," a loose-fitting cloak, to Shakespeare; but there did exist in Venice a garment (apart from the beret) that was peculiar to Jews.

I suggest that Shakespeare had heard that Jews in Venice were forced to wear something that would identify them, but perhaps got no account of what it was and so made up his own. In any case, the important point is that there *was* discrimination, and that Shakespeare makes it exist, too.

The very word "ghetto" originated in Venice. The Jews are forced to live in the ghetto and nowhere else, and they were literally locked in it every night. The final insult was that they had to furnish the money for the salary of the (Gentile) official who did the locking.[26] Jews were forbidden to own real estate in the city.[27] Shakespeare gives no hint that Shylock dwells in a specially designated quarter of the city, and he also seems to assume that Shylock owns his house. Either the dramatist did not know anything about the Ghetto, or he did not care to be factual on this point.

But Shakespeare does have Shylock dwelling in Venice itself, whereas in his source the Jewish moneylender dwells in Mestri, the nearest mainland town. In this case, both Shakespeare and Ser Giovanni are historically accurate. In the fourteenth century Jews were indeed forbidden to dwell in Venice itself, and they did indeed dwell in Mestri; but the Ghetto in Venice was founded in 1516, and the Jews had dwelt there ever since. We cannot know whether Shakespeare was accurate here by chance or by design, but he did go to the trouble to change the source when it would presumably have been easier to go along with it. He may have changed the source to avoid an extra scene shift, but he may also have done so because the Jew's situation is more poignant if he is portrayed as dwelling directly in the Christians' midst than if seen as dwelling in a separate town. The separate town would have symbolized Shylock's alien status, all right, but too blatantly.

Historically, economic discrimination against Jews in Venice was powerful. They had to pay disproportionately heavy taxes.[28] The number of occupations open to them was small: about all most were permitted to do was to loan money at interest and take pawn. If the goods were not redeemed by the appointed date, they were allowed to sell them, so that they were the leading second-hand dealers in the city (Sir Politic Would-be in *Volpone* says,"I . . . took me a house / Dealt with my Jews to furnish it with movables"—4.1.40–41). At least theoretically, interest could not rise above five percent, and a Gentile official lived in the Ghetto whose duty it was to see that the lists of pawns were just and that excessive interest was not charged "so that poor persons and women will not be tricked by the lenders."[29]

The Jews' assigned role as moneylenders must have fueled the kind of hatred of them that Shakespeare dramatizes by means of Antonio's attitude toward Shylock. Such hatred is based not only on religious belief (Christian doctrine forbade usury) but also on envy. We would expect that in historical Venice the Jews, in their turn, would have reacted to this hatred and envy with the kind of hatred that Shylock displays after Jessica elopes, though perhaps not to such an extreme degree. And indeed historical evidence indicates mutual enmity. For instance, the "Officers of night" for criminal matters ("Signore di notte criminali"), who combined the functions of night watchmen and police court, had specific jurisdiction over altercations between Christians and Jews—a power which presumably would not have been specified unless such incidents occurred fairly frequently.[30] And anecdotal evidence suggests that when the Venetian Jews were insulted in their own ghetto, they could be rather militant. During his 1608 visit to the ghetto, Coryat, eccentric as ever, ventured into the ghetto alone and began an argument about religion with a rabbi. The Odcombian continues:

> . . . after there had passed many vehement speeches to and fro betwixt us, it happened that some forty or fifty Jewes more flocked about me, and some of them beganne very insolently to swagger with me, because I durst reprehend their religion: Whereupon fearing least they would have offered me some violence, I withdrew my selfe by little and little towards the bridge at the entrance into the Ghetto, with an intent to flie from them, but by good fortune our noble Ambassador Sir Henry Wotton passing under the bridge in his Gondola at that very time, espyed me somewhat earnestly bickering with them, and so incontinently sent unto me out of his boate one of his principall Gentlemen . . . who conveighed mee safely from these unchristian miscreants. . . .(I.376)

Even though the chances are not great that Shakespeare knew much about the actual relations between Christians and Jews in Venice, there are many interesting parallels in this regard between history and play. The most general one is that in history and fiction relations seem—predominantly but by no means altogether—bad. Even if Jews were treated better in Venice than in other Christian places, and even though Jews could theoretically get equal justice in Venice, the ignominy of wearing special clothing, being locked in segregated quarters at night, and being virtually prevented from practicing all trades but one would have made hatred like Shylock's understandable. Similarly, in the play, the Christians' treatment of Shylock makes his hatred explicable, although the play does not justify the attempted murder of Antonio regardless of how much persecution the Jew has suffered.

Another similarity is that Shylock's hatred is complicated, just as doubtless a Jew's hatred in the real Venice would have been. Untangling Shylock's economic from his religious reasons for hating Antonio seems impossible. Although the Jew mentions religion first ("I hate him for he is a Christian"), he adds, "*But more* [emphasis mine], for that in low simplicity / He lends out money gratis, and brings down / The rate of usance here with us in Venice" (1.3.42–45). But in the next breath, he says bitterly, "He hates our sacred nation. . ." (1.3.48).

Christian prejudice against the Jews in the play is also complex. On the one hand, Antonio spits in Shylock's beard and calls him a dog; but on the other hand, the hatred seems to be religious as opposed to racial—Jessica, after all, is accepted by the Christians enthusiastically, and she is Shylock's flesh and blood.[31] Similarly, in sixteenth-century Venice, despite myriad ways in which Jews were discriminated against, there was nevertheless some cultural interchange. The modern historian Frederick Lane says that despite periods of anti-Semitism (as when many blamed the Jews for the gigantic explosion in the Arsenal in 1569), during the 1590s relations were so good that Christians and Jews were allowed to and did attend each other's musical and theatrical events.[32] Pullan has found considerable evidence of pleasant relationships between maverick Christians and the Jewish community.[33]

My conclusion from these comparisons is that if (as I suspect) Shakespeare knew little about actual Venetian Jews, he was nevertheless able to imagine a situation remarkably like the real thing—an amazing feat.

IV. What the Setting Does for the Play

The best way to sum up what Shakespeare does with the Venetian setting and why he does it is to contrast the use of setting in *Merchant* to the use of setting in a later problem comedy, *Measure for Measure.* Nothing in *Measure* connects the setting with the actual historical city of Vienna, whereas *Merchant* is fairly rich in details of local color. We hear, for instance, of gondolas and magnificos, of the Rialto and the "tranect."[34] More significantly, however, Shakespeare uses aspects of the Myth of Venice—particularly the alleged impartiality of the Venetian judiciary. This difference in the two plays is not to be attributed simply to the fact that Shakespeare obviously knew more about Venice than he did about Vienna. It is primarily, I think, because the Myth of Venice existed and was so powerful; and secondarily, because of differences in the two plots. In both plays, Shakespeare probably wanted the audience to feel a certain distance from the action and so he removes it (as is usual in his comedies) from England. But *Measure* has a more realistic plot (despite certain primitive devices like the Duke in Disguise and the bed trick) than *Merchant.* Hence there was less need to modernize the story by means of setting. Both the flesh-bond story and the main characters in it are so nearly akin to a fairy tale that even Ser Giovanni felt the need to make it more credible by setting it in the actual modern city of Venice, but he does not go much beyond that. As in many novellas, the characters are given a local habitation, but some get no name. Portia is called simply "la donna di Belmonte," while Shylock is called "il Giudeo." Shakespeare's play is a good deal more realistic and credible than Giovanni Fiorentino's story.

One of the most important critical issues of our time concerning the play is whether it is primarily a romantic comedy not far removed from its fairy-tale sources or a somber tragicomedy about contemporary issues.[35] My whole argument here would lead one to believe that I am strongly in the latter camp. Oddly enough, however, I am not. At the risk of seeming a fence-sitter, I would argue that the play's perennial popularity in the theater indicates that Shakespeare has been at least partially successful in having it both ways: he was able to retain some of the archetypal power of fairy tale, Biblical story, and melodrama, while at the same time giving his play the feel of contemporary, though exotic, events. This means that Antonio is both a fairly realistic Venetian merchant *and* "a tainted wether of the flock"; Shylock is both a somewhat realistic Venetian Jew *and* (for instance) The Miser. Bassanio is both the Prodigal Son *and* a Venetian turning landward. Portia plays a role analogous to God's in the Abraham and Isaac story (making the sacrifice unnecessary); yet she is also a marriageable heiress of the Veneto.

To recapitulate: how is Shakespeare able to have it both ways? Basically he does it by combining archetypally powerful stories with characters who are complex, magnetic and—to a considerable extent—credible. And their credibility arises in part from the Myth of Venice.

4
Othello and the Myth

Othello. I took you for that cunning whore of Venice
That married with Othello.

(4.2.89–90)

The myth of *Venezia-città-galante* may lie behind (far behind) Jessica's elopement and also Bassanio's prodigality in *The Merchant of Venice;* but it was not until *Othello* that Shakespeare made really crucial use of the sexual reputation of Venice. While that feature of the Myth is clearly the one most germane to *Othello,* the political and economic sides of the Myth are important too—in ways, I shall argue, which are not often stressed.[1] However, before getting into possible relationships between the Myth and the play, we should recall just how important the setting is in *Othello.*

I. "This is Venice": Shakespeare's Insistence on the Venetian Connection

"This is Venice," shouts Brabantio, "My house is not a grange" (1.1.105–06). While the main point of this line, as Kernan has argued,[2] is that Venice represents the city (that is, civilization), the line also serves to put the audience on notice in no uncertain terms, and near the outset, of the location of the action. I contend that the text keeps us in mind of Venice throughout, though of course much less often in the final four acts. Even in Cyprus, however, we hear fairly frequent reminders of the island's connections with Venice.

Let us begin with those bits of Venetian local color that were common knowledge and probably worked well precisely because they were. The fame of Venice as a republic meant (mainly because of ancient Rome) that the Senate got a lot of publicity. Only specialists in politics knew much about the Forty, the Ten, etc.; but almost everyone knew about the Senate. That fact gives ironic force to Iago's sarcastic reply to Brabantio: "You are—a senator" (1.1.118). The senators in the council scene (1.3) enjoy prominent roles, even if Shakespeare's Duke is apparently given more authority than the Doge actually possessed.[3] In Cyprus, Othello once remembers the Senate without even mentioning the Duke: "These letters give, Iago, to the pilot / And by him do my duties to the Senate" (3.2.1–2). When he speaks to Lodovico in 4.1, yet again he remembers the Senate. "The Duke and the senators of Venice greet you," Lodovico begins (4.1.217), a way of putting his greeting that stresses Venice's republican system. Othello's reply shows that he too is thinking of the system, since he mentions not the duke alone but the corporate body: "I kiss the instrument of *their* pleasures" (4.1.218—emphasis mine). Lodovico, reflecting (just after Othello's exit) on the Moor's strange behavior, reflects in senatorial terms: "Is this the noble Moor whom our full Senate / Call all in all sufficient?" (4.1.264–65). Even in Cyprus, then, the Senate's authority is very much felt and often mentioned.

Other common terms in the text show the author's general familiarity with Venetian polity and society. Othello refers to the Venetian government by its correct name, "the Signiory" (1.2.18); and Brabantio is called a "magnifico" (1.2.12), originally a term for a Venetian aristocrat, though it had attained the more general meaning of "great man" in Elizabethan English (see OED). Outside the governmental sphere one peculiarly Venetian term—then as now—immediately identifies the city: "gundolier" (1.1.125). Allusions to certain places in the Mediterranean world also serve as reminders of Venice. Rhodes and Cyprus were associated with Venice because they were both former possessions lost to the Turk in the sixteenth century; they are thus appropriate places for a Venetian veteran like Iago to have fought.[4] Othello's crucial allusion to Aleppo (5.2.352) calls Venice to mind because Aleppo had, in fact, for centuries been a major center for Venetian trade with turbaned Turks. Arthur Edwards mentions ". . . Aleppo, wherein continually are many Venetians dwelling, besides others that come yearly and there buy wools, . . . tallow, saffron, skins, cotton wooll, and other wares and great store of spices."[5]

In addition to these commonly known bits of local color are other allusions which are either (a) not *clearly* local color, or (b)

A Venetian Magnifico (left), the Doge in ceremonial attire (right). Volpone is a magnifico, and the Doge (called "Duke") is a character in both *Merchant of Venice* and *Othello*. From Abraham de Bruyn, *Omnium . . . Gentium Habitus* (Antwerp, 1581), Plate 30. By permission of the British Library.

A Moor with thick lips. When Roderigo calls Othello "the thick lips" (*Othello,* 1.1.66), he may be giving voice to a stereotype. The Moor in this picture, from Cesare Vecellio's *De gli habiti antichi, et moderni* (Venice, 1590), definitely has thick lips. See Sig. Qqq6 verso. By permission of the British Library.

based on facts not widely known. The problematic status of these allusions makes an investigation of them almost irresistible.

Roderigo's famous insult "the thick-lips" (1.1.66) is a case in point. There is just a chance that the epithet is in part a piece of Venetian (!) local color. In Vecellio both the 1590 and 1598 editions have a picture of a "noble Moor" ("Moro di conditione" in Italian, "Maurus nobilis" in Latin) who definitely has thick lips.[6] Vecellio may also provide a tiny bit of help with a still unsolved puzzle involving a location in Shakespeare's fictional Venice. When Iago directs Roderigo to bring the "raised" search "to the Sagittary," he is presumably naming an inn; but no inn called that has yet been found in historical records. For what it is worth, Vecellio's "Noble Moor" is pictured with a bow and arrows.[7]

The idea that the Venetians would appoint a foreigner to command an army is made much more plausible when one learns (reading Lewkenor, as Shakespeare himself probably did) that in Venice that practice was not merely permitted but was indeed customary: ". . . The Captaine Generall of our Armie . . . is alwaies a straunger."[8] The idea was to prevent military *coups d'etat:* "The Cittizens . . . of Venice for this reason are deprived of the honors belonging to warres by land and are contented to transferre them over to Straungers" (Lewkenor, Sig. S2v).

Another debate about Venetian local color turns upon a textual problem. At the close of the first scene, Brabantio, finally convinced that he should "get good guard and go along" with Roderigo, says that he will "raise some special officers. . . ." (1.1.182). The 1622 quarto adds "of night," whereas the folio reads "of might." If "of night" is the right reading, it is probably a reference to a particular kind of officer that Shakespeare could have read about in Lewkenor:

> . . . out of every tribe . . . is elected an officer of the night. . . . The duty of . . . these officers is, to keepe a watch . . . within their tribes and . . . to make rounds about his quarter, till the dawning of the day, being alwayes guarded and attended on with weaponed officers and serjeants, and to see that there be not any disorder done in the darkeness of the night. . . . (Sig. 0–0v)

The likelihood that Shakespeare noticed the description of these officers in Lewkenor is heightened slightly by the fact that the summary note in the margin reads "Officers of night."[9]

Moor with bow and arrows. In this engraving, as in one of a Moor by Vecellio, the figure is equipped with bow and arrows. Can this iconography be related to the "Sagittary" mentioned in *Othello* 1.1.158? From Jean Jacques Boissard, *Habitus Variarium Orbis Gentium* (Mechlin, 1581), Plate 59. By permission of the British Library.

Another interesting problem occurs at 1.2.12–14. Iago tells Othello that Brabantio "is much beloved, / And hath in his effect a voice potential / As double as the Duke's." Some editors interpret "double" simply as "strong," in which case there is no local color here at all. But if "double" has its literal meaning of "two," the text is probably alluding (though perhaps confusedly) to a report that the Doge had two votes under certain circumstances.[10]

Even an apparently neutral line such as "the general enemy Ottoman" (1.3.49) may conceal a specific allusion. The line clearly means "the enemy of all Christian commonwealths," but it may also allude to the fact that some Moorish kingdoms had been at war with the Turks at certain times during the sixteenth century. In fact, Moorish refugees from a Turkish attack on Tunis were brought to Venice in 1533.[11]

Research on *Volpone* reveals that Venetian mountebanks were the most famous of all mountebanks, and that fact may in turn give added point to Brabantio's complaint about the possibility that Othello has drugged Desdemona with "medicines bought of mountebanks" (1.3.61). Sansovino, discussing the complexion of Venetian women, says: ". . . [sono] bianchissime per natura" (1581 ed., Sig. Oo4), which calls to mind ". . . that whiter skin of hers than snow" (V.ii.4). Finally the emphasis on Cyprus as a "warlike isle" and a "town of war" stresses the combat with the Turks and hence Cyprus's connections with Venice.[12] Cyprus was a rough place because the Venetians used the wars there as an excuse to send undesirables to the island.[13]

When to the definite and common allusions are added some of the problematic ones (for surely at least *some* of the latter should be counted), the total is impressive. The text clearly insists, "This is Venice."

II. Of Arms and Beards: The Loss of Cyprus and the Myth of Venice

Why such an insistence on setting? One answer is that the political history of Venice may be a more important background for the play than has been generally recognized.

Shakespeare clearly used Richard Knolles's *General History of the Turks* (1603) in writing *Othello*.[14] The senators in the play are addressed by a messenger describing the Turkish movements:

Messenger. The Ottomites, reverend and gracious,
Steering with due course toward the isle of Rhodes,
Have there injointed them with an after fleet.

1. *Senator.* Ay, so I thought. How many, as you guess?

Messenger. Of thirty sail; and now they do restem
Their backward course, bearing with frank appearance
Their purposes toward Cyprus.

(1.3.33–39)

These movements "correspond exactly to Knolles's account of the Turkish invasion plans" during their defeat of the Venetians and conquest of Cyprus in 1570–1571.[15] Knolles says that Mustapha Bassa, commander of the expedition, arranged a rendezvous with a subordinate at Rhodes, "that he that came first should tarrie for the other, that so they might togither saile into CYPRUS" (Sig. Cccc3v). Knolles adds that the plan was carried out and that "the whole fleet at that time consisted of two hundred gallies." The last report that the senators in *Othello* get on Turkish strength is two hundred galleys (1.3.4). The number could be a coincidence, but it is extremely difficult to believe that the similarity in tactical plans is too.[16]

Other features of the play are perhaps borrowed from Knolles. The idea for the storm in 2.1, for instance, may have come not only from the fate of the Spanish Armada in '88, but also from the following passage on the Cyprus campaign: "Now all the hope of the Christians, was to have kept the Turkes from landing . . . knowing in the meane time, that in all the island was no good harbour for them to put into, and that riding in an open road subject to all wind and weather, they could not long without danger of shipwracke ride it out" (Sig. Cccc4). Mustapha was said by Knolles to have forty thousand pioneers at the siege of Famagusta (Sig. Dddd6); this gives added hideousness to Othello's "I had been happy, if the general camp, / Pioners and all, had tasted her sweet body, / So I had nothing known" (3.3.345–47).

The use to which Jones puts the idea that Shakespeare was indebted to Knolles is sound in some ways but questionable in others. He argues that Shakespeare's use of the Turkish/Cypriot material is connected with King James, and that the connection is to be found in the King's long poem on the battle of Lepanto (written ca. 1585; published, 1591; reprinted London, 1603). The battle, famous because really notable victories over the Turk were scarce in the sixteenth century, was celebrated by the young poet/

prince despite the thorny religious issue involved (all of the Christian forces—Venetian, Spanish, Papal—were unfortunately Catholic). The Christian coalition was an uneasy one that would probably never have coalesced at all except for the Turkish invasion of Cyprus, a truly crucial Venetial outpost.

Jones points out that while the Cypriot setting is in Shakespeare's main source (Cinthio's novella), the island in the novella is at peace. The whole notion of the war with the Turks must have come from somewhere, and surely Knolles is the likeliest source (in view of the correspondences in details noted above).

Against Jones's thesis that Shakespeare wrote about the war because of the King's interest in the Battle of Lepanto, one might argue that the play makes no mention of Lepanto and that (ac-

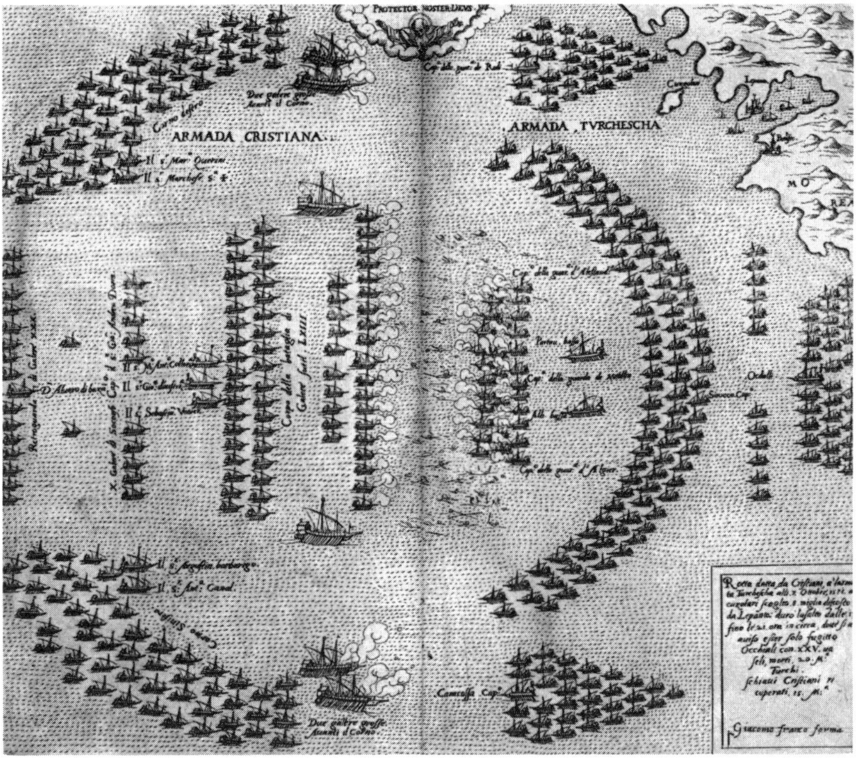

Battle formations of the Christian and Turkish fleets at Lepanto. The Venetians were extremely proud of the role which their men and ships played at Lepanto. From Giacomo Franco, *Habiti d'huomeni* [*sic*] *et donne Venetiani* (Venice, c. 1609), Plate 33. By permission of the British Library.

cording to Jones) there are "no specific reminiscences of the poem" in the play. As it happens, however, I think that I have found one such "specific reminiscence" that Professor Jones has overlooked. The King's opening verse paragraph announces his subject in epic fashion as "a bloodie battell bolde":

> Which fought was in LEPANTOES gulfe
> Betwixt the baptiz'd race,
> And circumsised Turband Turkes
> Rencountring in that place.[17]

Shakespeare is probably alluding to the line "circumsised Turband Turkes" in Othello's suicide speech:

> And say besides, that in Aleppo once,
> Where a malignant and a *turban'd Turk*
> Beat a Venetian and traduc'd the state,
> I took by th'throat the *circumcised* dog,
> And smote him—thus.
> (5.2.352–56, italics mine)

Of course both "turban'd" and "circumsised" were adjectives applied frequently to Turks in Shakespeare's day, but the use of both in such proximity to one another suggests that this may be a "specific reminiscence."

To me, however, the biggest difficulty with Jones's thesis is not that the verbal connections between play and poem are tenuous (or, as he would have it, nonexistent), but that his thesis is based to some extent on a questionable assumption. Like those who argue for a resemblance between the Duke in *Measure for Measure* and King James, Jones seems to assume that the mere treatment by a playwright of a subject in which the king was known to be interested would have constituted a compliment to the king. While this may be true at the most superficial level, surely much depends on how the playwright treats the subject. The portrait of the Duke in *Measure* is not entirely flattering; what of the issues which that circumstance raises? Similarly, it may be that Shakespeare has used the idea of Turkish invasion partly because of the king's poem; but there are implications in such a theory which no Christian king or (for that matter) citizen could have found pleasant.

For if Shakespeare read the passages in Knolles already cited, he could also have read the following one:

> In the middest of all this joy, generally conceived of the late victorie [at Lepanto], one of the cheefe prisoners of the Turks, hearing it compared with the losse of CYPRUS (for that *Selymus* had therin lost his fleet, his best men of warre, with great store of ordinance) by a fit comparison shewed it not to be so, saying, That the battell lost, was unto *Selymus* as if a man should shave his beard, which would ere long grow againe; but that the losse of CYPRUS was unto the Venetians, as the losse of an arme, which once cut off, could never be againe recovered. Declaring thereby the great inequaltie of the losse. (Sig. F fff 5)

Just as the meaning of a given passage in Shakespeare's history plays is conditioned by the audience's knowledge of the historical outcome of that episode, so the knowledge possessed by some at the Globe in 1603 that Cyprus had, in fact, been in Turkish hands for some thirty-two years (and that there was no apparent prospect of recapturing it) is a part of the meaning of *Othello.* Chances are good that many had heard of the loss. For instance, Nestore Martinengo's account of the most crucial battle, published at Verona in 1572, was translated the same year and published as *The True Report of all the successe of Famagosta.* Previous critics have not given sufficient attention to the pessimistic implications of the *loss* of Cyprus.[18]

Alvin Kernan, for instance, is aware of the dark side of the Myth of Venice (my terminology, of course, not his) but chooses to stress the bright side:

> Renaissance Venice was known for its wealth acquired by trade, its political cunning, and its courtesans; but Shakespeare, while reminding us of the tradition of the "supersubtle Venetian," makes Venice over into a form of *The City,* the ageless image of government, of reason, of law, and of social concord.[19]

As I hope my chapter on the Myth has shown, it was not necessary that Shakespeare "make Venice over"; it was only necessary that he dwell on the bright rather than the dark side of the Myth.

And dwell Shakespeare does—but only on the surface. As Kernan argues, the image of the Signiory in 1.3 is highly favorable. Because Brabantio is a powerful magnifico, Iago warns Othello, the senator may prevail at the hearing. But Brabantio does not prevail. Whatever their motives (more on that later), the Duke and senators give Othello and Desdemona a fair hearing and rule in their favor. Since we ourselves doubt the witchcraft charge, we are pleased by the decision. With regard to the Turks, too, the senators show excellent judgment, again expressed well by Kernan:

> . . . the clear mind of the Senate probes the actions of the Turks, penetrates through their pretenses to their true purposes, makes sense of the frantic and fearful contradictory messages which pour in from the fleet, and arranges the defense.[20]

Kernan also notes that the very costumes of the senators make an impression on us in productions, their splendor signifying the power and authority of *La Serenissima.*

But in a sense, as Lear puts it, "Robes and furred gowns hide all." The most obvious shadow looming over 1.3 (a shadow that Kernan ignores) is that the motives of the Duke and senators are mixed. It is fair enough to image their acting partly out of concern to uphold Venice's reputation for justice to foreigners (the idea on which Shylock placed—ironically in view of the outcome—so much reliance). It is equally clear that they are also acting from self-interest: the "trade and profit of the city" (*Merchant,* 3.3.30) required that Venice retain Cyprus. As Knolles says, the island "aboundeth with corne, wine, oyle, cotton wooll, saffron, honey, rosin, turpentine, sugar canes. . . ." (Sig. Cccc2). Iago's prediction on the outcome of the hearing is suffused with *realpolitik:*

> . . . for I do know the state,
> (How ever this may gall him with some check)
> Cannot with safety cast him, for he's embark'd
> With such loud reason to the Cyprus wars
> (Which even now stands in act) that for their souls,
> Another of his fadom they have none
> To lead their business. . . .
> (1.1.147–53)

Othello, more idealistic, thinks that he will win before the senators because of his past (not future) services: "My services which I have done the signiory / Shall out-tongue his complaints" (1.2.18–19). But even *he* does not mention the Signiory's reputation for justice. While we would be foolish to condemn good results merely because they come out of mixed motives, we can nevertheless sense the Venetian will to power behind the just decision and should not ignore it.

Furthermore, the wisdom of the Signiory looks rather different if we put the Senate scene in its historical context. As pointed out earlier, Cyprus had been in Turkish hands for thirty-two years and, perhaps more important, there was no prospect of regaining it. Indeed, the Turk had regrown his beard and had gained still more territory in the interim. It was a classic case of winning the battle (Lepanto) but losing the war. I repeat that those in the audience who knew of the fall of Cyprus must have found the Senate scene ironic.

The same can be said of the early scenes in Cyprus. The enchafed flood has swallowed up the Turks, as it had the Spanish Armada, and as the Third Gentleman says, "our wars are done" (2.1.20). On his arrival, Othello confirms the joyful news: "The Turks are drown'd," (2.1.202); and "the mere perdition of the Turkish fleet" is made the occasion for "full liberty of feasting" (2.2.3, 9). The proclamation ends with a suggestive linkage: "[Heaven] bless the isle of Cyprus and our noble general Othello!" (9–12). In the back of the knowledgeable playgoer's mind must have been the notion that from a Christian point of view Cyprus had not been much blessed for the past thirty-two years, and that that idea perhaps had ominous implications for our noble general Othello.

Lilian Winstanley long ago argued that *Othello* is actually an historical allegory in which Othello, with his Moorishness, represents Spain and Desdemona represents Venice murdered by Spain and the Pope.[21] Though ingenious, as the best such readings always are, it is, of course, so reductive as to be absurd. In suggesting an analogy between the loss of Cyprus historically and Othello's loss of Desdemona, I seem to be following in Winstanley's footsteps; but I suggest merely that the play is more unified and impressive if we see that the political background imported by Shakespeare into Cinthio's story is perhaps more significant than has generally been realized. Shakespeare rather insists on the Venetian and Cypriot settings, and the Decline of Venice is an important context for the Decline of Othello.

III. "Our country disposition": *Othello* and the Sexual Reputation of Venice

1. IAGO

"I know our country disposition well," says Iago in the temptation scene: "In Venice they do let [God] see the pranks / They dare not show their husbands; their best conscience, / Is not to leave't undone, but keep't unknown" (3.3.201–04). He is craftily using the dark side of the myth of *Venezia-città-galante.*

As he gives voice to the Myth, he is in a sense a product of it. Foreign critics of Venice claimed that the large conscience that Venice had below the navel resulted from the education given the young men in the city, and Iago has been shaped by this education. William Thomas complains:

> But surely many of them trade and bring up their children in so much liberty that one is no sooner out of the shell but he is hail fellow with father and friend, and by that time he cometh to twenty years of age, he knoweth as much lewdness as is possible to be imagined. For his greatest exercise is to go amongst his companions to this good woman's house and that, of which in Venice are many thousands of ordinary less than honest. (p. 82)

Amelot de la Houssaye asserts, ". . . 'tis a common thing to see the Father courting his Concubine, and treating the other instruments of his Debauchery in the presence of his Son, who perhaps learns the act, before he understands the evil. . . ."[22] Mission even claims that mothers had been known to conclude the financial agreements with their sons' courtesans (II.656, Col. 2).

Iago is a true son of his native land, or at least of the negative stereotype of his native land. Because his own mind is so inveterately pornographic, he is able to use pornography to manipulate other characters. Othello is only the most notable of these; Iago also uses this weapon on Brabantio. The magnifico first answers to the "terrible summons" of Iago and Roderigo in the opening scene sleepily and confusedly; but he becomes more attentive after Iago's graphic imagery of the old black ram tupping the white ewe and the devil making a grandsire of him. On discovering Roderigo's name, however, Brabantio's interest wanes; and he is unimpressed by the gull's relatively polite protestations. We may imagine that he is even considering going back to bed. To the rescue, Iago's pornography: ". . . you'll have your daughter cover'd with a Barbary horse, you'll have your nephews neigh to you; you'll have coursers for cousins, and gennets for germans" (1.1.111–13). Brabantio, his interest caught, inquires, "What profane wretch art thou?" Iago typically answers with yet another graphic sexual image: ". . . your daughter and the Moor are [now] making the beast with two backs."

Iago nearly always uses sexual imagery to manipulate Roderigo. He urges Roderigo, "And though he in a fertile climate dwell,

/ Plague him with flies" (1.1.70–71). The main effect of his steamy imagery is to make Roderigo angry enough to disturb Brabantio, but surely Roderigo is also imagining himself as dwelling in the fertile climate instead of Othello. The same technique works in persuading Roderigo to join the first plot against Cassio. The Ancient re-creates the scene in which Cassio was kissing Desdemona's hand:

> Lechery, by this hand; an index and obscure prologue to the history of lust and foul thoughts. They met so near with their lips that their breaths embrac'd together. . . . When these [mutualities] so marshal the way, hard at hand comes the master and main exercise, th'incorporate conclusion. (2.1.257–63)

One does not have to be an experienced consumer of commercial pornography to recognize the pattern here: from foreplay to coition itself, from dalliance to climax.

It is as if Iago had merely been practicing on Roderigo; he uses pornography brilliantly to manipulate Othello. He ostensibly argues that he cannot arrange for Othello to "behold her topped" (3.3.396), but his word picture is so powerful that in effect Othello does "see" them in the act:

> It were a tedious difficulty, I think,
> To bring them to that prospect; damn them then,
> If ever mortal eyes do see them bolster
> More than their own! What then? How then?
> What shall I say? Where's satisfaction?
> It is impossible you should see this,
> Were they as prime as goats, as hot as monkeys,
> As salt as wolves in pride, and fools as gross
> As ignorance made drunk.
> (3.3.397–405)

That Iago's imagery has lodged in Othello's mind and is festering is indicated by the Moor's later involuntary eruption "Goats, and monkeys!" (4.1.263).

Iago's greatest pornographic masterpiece, however, is his account of the night he spent with Cassio. This dirty fiction is replete with dialogue, even:

> In sleep I heard him say, "Sweet Desdemona,
> Let us be wary, let us hide our loves";

> And then, sir, would he gripe and wring my hand;
> Cry, "O sweet creature!" then kiss me hard,
> As if he pluck'd up kisses by the roots
> That grew upon my lips; [then] laid his leg
> [Over] my thigh, and [sigh'd], and [kiss'd], and then
> [Cried], "Cursed fate that gave thee to the Moor!"
> (3.3.419–26)

In sum, Iago's pornography does much to drive the plot, and Iago's pornographic habits of mind are more comprehensible against the background of the negative stereotypes about the education of young men in Venice.

2. OTHELLO

In addition to the wicked Iago, Othello had two stereotypes operating against him: there is some evidence that Moors had a reputation for being especially jealous of their wives, and a great deal of evidence that Venetians did too. Both heredity and environment—one might say—were against him. Draper mentions the jealousy of Moors,[23] and testimony to the jealousy of Venetians is plentiful. A French traveler early in the sixteenth century, Jacques Le Saige, tells of seeing two beautiful women at church on Ascension Day. He comments, "For the rest of the days all year long they are in a high chamber. . . . Their husbands are so jealous of them. . . ."[24]

Coryat puts this stereotype in his own inimitable way. He speaks of the condition of being "capricornified (which of all the indignities in the world the Venetian cannot patiently endure). . . ."[25] Moryson claims that because of jealousy Venetian men "dare not trust men servants with their wives and daughters."[26]

This stereotype persisted into the late seventeenth century. In 1699, St. Didier's English translator waxes indignant:

> Yet there are those who allow their Wives no farther Liberty than to perform their Devotions in the nearest Church to them. Some carry this excess of Jealousie to a higher degree, who without any scruple make their own Houses their Wives Prisons, from whence they are never permitted to stir.[27]

St. Didier adds, "Of six or seven Hundred Ladies of *Venice,* there are not above fifty or sixty that appear at Church at a time, or any where Publickly" (Part 3, p. 19). A historian of Venice at the turn of the twentieth century quotes St. Didier's statistics and suggests that the idea of confining wives may have come to Venice from Byzantium.[28] Historians have unearthed the story of a murder motivated by jealousy in Venice in 1602 that bears a certain resemblance to *Othello.* One Lucrezia Sanudo was slain 11 July 1602. Domenico Bollani, Bishop of Canea, describes public reaction as follows:

> One of the Sanudo family that lives on the Rio della Croce on the Giudecca made his wife go to Confession the other day . . ., and, the night following, about five o'clock, he stabbed her in the throat and killed her: it is said it was because she was not faithful to him, but the neighborhood spoke of her as a saint.[29]

Was Othello "not easily jealous"? Many have doubted his statement.[30] Seen against the background of the stereotype of Venetian husbands, his anguished self-justification does not seem quite so hard to accept.

3. BIANCA

Shakespeare takes full advantage of Venice's reputation for courtesans by developing Bianca, whose counterpart in Cinthio gets only a sentence or two (and is not a courtesan). Bianca is a minor, but still fascinating, figure. She is on stage for only fifty lines and is the primary topic of conversation in another fifty or so; yet she serves some important functions.

She should not be regarded as one of the rich courtesans mentioned by Coryat, the kind who founded hospitals and lived in "Palaces (as indeed some few of the principallest of them live in very magnificent and portly buildings fit for the entertainement of a great Prince)" (1.403). Nor, at the other extreme, does she seem to be one of those whom Coryat says "open their quivers to every arrow" (1.402). But Cassio, who seems a decent enough fellow in most respects, laughs heartily at the story that he is planning to marry her, a mere "customer" (4.1.119), an indication of her status.

Bianca, then, was probably an average courtesan; and as it happens, there was just such a courtesan in Venice named Bianca about the time of the play *Othello.* The chances that Shakespeare knew of her are almost infinitesimal. After all, he was doubtless attracted to the name because of its ironic connotations of purity; and with thousands of prostitutes in the city, it would have been surprising if there had *not* been one named Bianca.[31] Nevertheless, on the list of "public whores condemned for transgression of the laws" from 1579 to 1617, we find "La signora Biancha" fined ten ducats on 10 February 1596 and thirty ducats on 2 December 1602.[32]

Bianca's most important function is to serve as a powerful contrast to the chaste Desdemona, especially considering that Othello in 4.2 treates his wife as if she too were a mere "customer." Desdemona is not a "cunning whore of Venice," but Bianca is. The contrast is crucial. The existence of Bianca enriches the meaning of Desdemona's purity, and the reputation of both women is more clearly understood in the light of the city's reputation for whores.

4. DESDEMONA

Vecellio tells a story that helps to explain how the reputation of Venice for courtesans rubbed off to some extent on the decent women of the city. He says that some of the higher-class courtesans, when they had been the mistress of a noble Venetian for a considerable time, often had the nerve to assume the last name of their protector, and by this means occasionally convinced foreigners that they were themselves members of the most noble families in Venice. Vecellio adds that most of the foreigners who went around bragging that they had enjoyed the favors of Venetian gentlewomen were victims of this confidence game, "since commonly Venetian gentlewomen are very jealous of their honor and are mirrors of honesty and modesty."[33]

Vecellio is guilty of special pleading, since Venetian gentlewomen were doubtless the main market for his book. Yet he is not altogether off the mark. Venetian wives could not possibly have strayed much because they were watched so warily. If wives and daughters were indeed kept virtual prisoners, as most travelers believed, then it is easy to understand Desdemona's naiveté.

For Desdemona is extremely naive. We can believe that she has been faithful and has never even thought of straying. But it is difficult to suspend disbelief when she asks, "Dost thou in conscience think—tell me, Emilia— / That there be women do abuse their husbands / In such gross kind?" (4.3.61–63). This is staggeringly naive.

How are we to reconcile this naiveté with the boldness that she displays in the Senate scene? One way is to look toward the Venetian background of the play. The naiveté, as already pointed out, is explicable in light of the idea that wives and daughters were kept cloistered. The boldness may be explicable in light of Venetian education for a few privileged women. Margaret King has shown that the humanist movement reached a tiny proportion of aristocratic Venetian women in the fifteenth century,[34] and we may presume that the habit of giving a humanist education to an occasional daughter of the Clarissimi continued into the sixteenth century as well. There was strong prejudice against educating women, of course; indeed, one malicious male accused a learned woman of incest and added that he agreed with the many wise men who held that an eloquent woman was never chaste.[35] The Venetian Senate itself, however, chose Cassandra Fedele to pen an oration in honor of the visiting Queen of Poland in 1556.[36]

We may doubt whether Shakespeare knew much about the education of Venetian women; but such information may sometimes be transmitted via lowbrow books (novellas) as well as by highbrow books (learned treatises). I have a suggestion as to one medium through which the idea of Venetian gentlewomen speaking eloquently might have reached Shakespeare. William Painter's *Palace of Pleasure* contains a story, "Two Gentlewomen of Venice," that features such an incident. The chances that Shakespeare might have read this story, and that it might have influenced his handling of 1.3, seem to me great enough to merit an extended examination of this novella and its possible relationships to the play.

The story, originally by Bandello, was translated into French and thence into English.[37] We can be reasonably sure that Shakespeare had access to it because it comes in *The Palace of Pleasure* immediately after Painter's version of the Romeo and Juliet story, a version which (it is generally agreed)[38] Shakespeare had probably read. Those aspects of the plot of "Two Gentlewomen" that are relevant to my arguments may be summarized as follows:

> Two noble Venetians marry wives who are long-time friends. Each falls in love with the other's wife, but the "subtill dames" pull the old bed trick (doubled): each man is sleeping with his own wife, but thinks he is committing adultery. One night during a commotion caused by someone else the two Venetians are apprehended—nearly nude and in the wrong beds—by the Officers of Night. Thrown into adjacent cells, they compare notes; each decides that he is a cuckold.

> Despondent and desiring to commit a kind of suicide, they falsely confess to have murdered the Duke's nephew. But the Duke figures out that their confession is false. To arrive at the truth publicly he condemns the gentlemen to death, though he has no intention of carrying out the sentences. The two wives then ask for a public hearing before the Council and there, in order to save their husbands' lives, they confess their trickery. One of the wives, Mistress Isotta, delivers an eloquent oration before the Council in which she argues at great length that all the turmoil is due to the infidelity of their husbands—that it is just as bad for husbands to be unfaithful as it is for wives to do so.[39] The husbands gladly endure this energetic and protracted feminist lecture because they are so happy to discover they are not cuckolds after all. The couples are reconciled.

Painter calls attention to the speech by special mention in the heading:

> *Two gentlemen of Venice were honourably deceived of their Wyves, whose notable practises, and secret conference for atchievinge their desire, occasioned divers accidentes, and ingendred double benefit: wherein also is recited an eloquent oration, made by one of them, pronounced before the Duke and the state of that Cittye. . . .* (p. 125)

The stage is set for Mistress Isotta's speech by the ravings of her jealous husband, who somewhat resembles Othello after the latter's transformation:

> Anselmo more angry and impacient then Girolamo, brake out into sutch furie, as had it not ben for the majesty of the place, and the Companye of People to have stayed him, woulde have kylled them: and seyng he was not able to hurt them, he began to utter the vylest Woords, that he possibly could devise agaynst them. (p. 146)

We think of the scene (4.2.24–94) in which Othello "bewhores" his wife as brutal, but at least it takes place in private rather than in public.

Mistress Isotta's eloquence in the face of her husband's bitter denunciation is stressed by the narrator. At the outset we are told that she "conceived courage, and cravinge licence of the Duke to speake, with merrye countenance and good uttrance began . . . to say her mind" (p. 146). Similarly, at the close of the speech we are told that the "Parents, Cosins, and Friends of the husbands and wyves . . . greatly praysed the maner of their delivery, accoumpting the women to be very wise, and mistresse Isotta to be an eloquent gentlewoman. . . ." (p. 152).

Isotta's speech may be eloquent, but it does not have the virtue of brevity. The modern reader tends to want her to hurry up and get to the point. Desdemona, by contrast, is admirably brief: she speaks only three times, for a total of some twenty-seven verse lines, in the whole Council scene. Yet she, like Isotta, is (to my mind) quite eloquent. The rhetorical balance in her first speech (1.3.180–89) between the expressions of gratitude to her father and the pledges of fidelity to her husband is admirable, and her argument is the stronger for being based on biblical authority: "For this cause shall a man leave father and mother, and shall cleave to his wife: and they twain shall be one flesh."[40] Skipping to her third speech, we are impressed by the vividness of her metaphors:

> That I [did] love the Moor to live with him,
> My downright violence, and storm of fortunes,
> May trumpet to the world. My heart's subdu'd
> Even to the very quality of my lord.
> I saw Othello's visage in his mind,
> And to his honors and his valiant parts
> Did I my soul and fortunes consecrate.
> (1.3.248–54)

Both Isotta and Desdemona are eloquent and bold in speaking out before a Venetian Council (Painter's Council and Shakespeare's may not be precisely the same body, technically speaking; but it would not be to the purpose here to go into the intricacies of Venetian polity). Isotta observes the proprieties of that era by apologizing that she, a mere woman, is addressing them:

> . . . I will assay . . . although it be not appropriate to our kind in publike place to declayme, nor yet to open sutch bold attempts, but that necessity of matter and oportunity of time, and place dothe bolden us to enter into these termes, whereof we crave a thousand pardons for our unkindely dealings, and render double thanks to your honours, for admitting us to speake. (p. 146–47)

Desdemona too is apologetic to the Duke: "Most gracious Duke, / To my unfolding lend your prosperous ear, / And let me find a charter in your voice / T'assist my simpleness" (1.3.243–46). She does not bring up the issue of the alleged inappropriateness of women addressing the Council, but her allusion to her "simpleness" may hint at it. In any case, the boldness displayed by Isotta before an august body of Venetians may have suggested to Shakespeare the boldness that Desdemona displays before a similar Venetian body.

Which is the "real" Desdemona: the bold speaker before the Council, or the naive sheltered girl? If we look at her with the aid of the Myth of Venice, both Desdemonas are believable. Indeed, they are one and the same, and her character appears reasonably consistent throughout.

IV. A Sense of Doom in *Othello*

The common thread connecting the political and sexual uses of the Myth in *Othello* is that both add a sense of impending doom. The fall of the real, as opposed to the fictional, Cyprus was not a possibility but a *fait accompli;* and the fall of the real Cyprus in a sense foreshadows the fall of Othello himself: both are attached to Venice but both meet their downfall—one through the machinations of the Turks, the other through the machinations of Iago—although both the island and the Moor are ripe for the picking. As for the sexual reputation of Venice, the characters seen against it are more understandable but also more helpless, more easily prey to the forces of their social environment.

Othello does not have anything like the same power in its sense of doom that the witches add to *Macbeth,* and yet there are parallels. Macbeth *has* free will and yet, paradoxically, he and the whole cast are in the grip of demonic powers; Othello, similarly, does not *have* to be jealous and yet, paradoxically, he and the whole cast are in the grip, to some extent, of a subtle kind of cultural determinism. As great and exceptional a hero as Othello is, he cannot singlehandedly battle the Myth of Venice and win.

Several critics have pointed out the striking similarities between portions of the plot of *Othello* and the structure of comedy.[41] Yet we would never mistake the play for a comedy. Iago's dark predictions do more than anything to keep the tone from becoming too light, but we should not overlook the subtle contribution of the Venetian background toward the same end.

5

Theatricality and the Myth of Venice in *Volpone*

> *Volpone.* As when in that so celebrated scene
> At recitation of our comedy
> For entertainment of the great Valois,
> I acted young Antinöus. . . .
>
> (3.7.159–62)

As Sugden observes, *Volpone* contains more details about Venice than does any other play of the period.[1] The same facet of Ben Jonson's character that drove him toward "integrity in the [hi]story" in *Sejanus* drove him toward very frequent and very accurate use of Venetian local color. I see no need, as in the case of *Othello,* to argue that the text insists upon its setting; it clearly does.

Nor is there need to argue for the general importance of the Myth of Venice to the play. Probably because of the continual and accurate references to the city in the text, this general importance has been more thoroughly investigated than it has in *Merchant* and *Othello.*[2] I am thinking particularly of the excellent work by two recent editors, John W. Creaser and R. B. Parker. Creaser is especially good at reading the English travel writers to get an understanding of Sir Politic Would-be,[3] but he largely confines himself to sources in English. Parker adds to Creaser's insights on the Italian background in general, using sources in several languages. He is clearly right, for instance, in concluding that of all great British writers, Jonson had the most Venetian sensibility.[4]

Since the general importance has been studied already, I have decided to approach this play on a somewhat more specialized level: the theatricality in the play as it relates to the Myth. Because of the fine work by Alvin Kernan, Jonas Barish, and others, theatricality in *Volpone* has already (like the general importance of the Myth) been well studied.[5] What I do *not* find is any attempt to link the two areas of study.

While most passages in Jonson's *Discoveries* are borrowed, no source has yet been found for the following one:

> *I have* considered, our whole life is like a *Play:* wherein every man, forgetfull of himselfe, is in travaile with expression of another. Nay, wee so insist in imitating others, as wee cannot (when it is necessary) returne to our selves. . . . (H&S ed., VIII.597, 11. 1093–96)

Jonson, believing as he did in the idea of the centered self,[6] dramatizes this concept in *Volpone.* Volpone plays three roles: sick magnifico, mountebank, and *commandatore.* In the end he is forced by the *Avocatori* not to feign but to *be* a sick magnifico:

> And since the most was gotten by imposture,
> By feigning lame, gout, palsy, and such diseases,
> Thou art to lie in prison, cramped with irons,
> Till thou beest sick and lame indeed.
> (5.7.121–24)

Whatever Volpone's future spiritual journey may be, he will never return to his ordinary social role in Venice: (physically) healthy magnifico.

I suggest here that there is a level to his role playing that has not as yet been fully recognized. Between his real (or in any case ordinary) self, the healthy magnifico, and the role of sick old man bilking legacy hunters, there is, I think, another role sandwiched: Volpone often imagines himself as a character in Imperial Rome—say, as Eumolpus, the witty, poetic, and unprincipled con man in *The Satyricon.* Volpone is very much aware that he is a part of the Venice of his own day; but, like Miniver Cheevy, he fantasizes about a world from the past: the world of Imperial Rome. I will show, first, that Volpone so insists on imitating the Roman world that he is almost unable to return to himself, and, second, that Sir Politic and his wife try so hard to imitate Venetians that they are in fact unable to return to themselves. They are imitators imitating an imitation: Britons aping a Venetian who is aping an ancient Roman.[7]

Venetian neoclassicism and love of ceremony. The Doge and his entourage visit the magnificent Palladian church of San' Giorgio Maggiore on Christmas Day. Both the neoclassical architecture and the elaborateness of Venetian rituals are illustrated here. From Giacomo Franco, *Habiti d'huomeni* [*sic*] *et donne Venetiani* (Venice, c. 1609), Plate 43. By permission of the British Library.

I. Background on the Settings

If Volpone imagines himself as Eumolpus or someone similar (and I will show later—in great detail—why I think he does), it is easy to see how he arrived at the idea. As early as 1077, Pope Gregory VII attributed the liberty of the Venetians to their supposed roots in the ancient Roman nobility.[8] Many sixteenth- and seventeenth-century writers influenced by the positive side of the Myth of Venice claimed that the soul of ancient Rome had transmigrated into Venice. The germ of the idea is in a Latin poem by Julius Caesar Scaliger, one of Jonson's favorite Renaissance critics. Scaliger evokes the horror of the Barbarian invasions of Rome, but asserts that the Roman genius nevertheless was reborn in the midst of the sea (that is, in Venice).[9] Several later writers pick up Scaliger's idea and develop it.

Protestant Englishmen were especially fond of comparing ancient Rome and modern Venice in order to put down, implicitly or explicitly, modern Rome and all it stood for. For example, in the address "To the Reader" of his translation of Thomas de Fougasses' *The Generall Historie of the Magnificent State of Venice,* W. Shute writes:

> . . . the *Genius* of it [ancient Rome] made transmigration to *Venice.* In her the Wisedom, Fortitude, Justice, and Magnanimitie of old *Rome* doe yet move and stirre. That which now Usurps that name is not *Rome,* but her Carkasse, or rather Sepulcher. All but her Ruines, and the Cause of them, (her Vice) is removed to *Venice.*[10]

The Scotsman William Lithgow, another fervent Protestant, copied the metaphor: ". . . the *Romane Genius* made a Pithagoricall transmigration into *Venice.*"[11]

James Howell, that Son of Ben, lacks the anti-Catholic bias but still uses the idea of Venice as Rome reborn. His pamphlet *S.PQ.V.* is an obvious allusion to *S.PQ.R.* He even goes into a tediously detailed comparison of the governmental bodies of the two republics (the Decemviri vs. the Council of Ten, etc.) and by valiantly straining finds seven ways in which modern Venice is actually superior to ancient Rome (*S.PQ.V.,* pp. 205–07 [Sig. Ee4–Ff]). John Raymond, an English travel writer, comments:

> This very mirrour of State and Policy, as she was borne about the death of old *Rome;* so shee seemes to bee hereditarily Possessour

> of that which maintained *Rome* in her soveraigne glory; The magnificent Genius of the People, the Gravity of the Senate, the solidity of her lawes, very much consonant with those of *Rome.*[12]

But these panegyrics conspicuously fail to mention the aspect of the Myth of Venice that interested Jonson most: *Venezia-città-galante.* Time and again in *Volpone* we either hear directly or are reminded indirectly of Venice as the pleasure capital of Europe. In this, too, I think, the soul of Rome had transmigrated into Venice. The three ways in which the reputations of the two empires as pleasure centers are alike all have to do in differing degrees with theatricality. The patricians in both empires had reputations for being extremely fond of lavish display and festivities, for loving theater itself, and for being given to exhibitionism in indulging their sexual passions—which they did obsessively.

1. EXCESSES IN IMPERIAL ROME

Suetonius, something of a sensationalist, is full of examples of the lavishness, theatricality, and sexual exhibitionism of Caligula and Nero. Of Caligula he writes:

> In reckless extravagance he outdid the prodigals of all times in ingenuity . . . for he would bathe in hot or cold perfumed oils, drink pearls of great price dissolved in vinegar, and set before his guests loaves and meats of gold, declaring that a man ought to be frugal or Caesar.[13] He even scattered large sums of money among the commons from the roof of the basilica Julia for several days in succession. . . .[14]

Nero imitated Caligula in lavishness:

> Nothing in his uncle Gaius so excited his envy and admiration as the fact that he had in so short a time run through the vast wealth which Tiberius had left him. . . . He [Nero] played at dice for four hundred thousand sesterces a point. He fished with a golden net drawn by cords woven of purple and scarlet threads. It is said that he never made a journey with less than a thousand carriages, his mules shod with silver. . . . (*Suetonius* II. 135)

Caligula and Nero were also the emperors who were participants in, as well as patrons of, theater. Caligula "exhibited stage-plays continually, of various kinds and in many different places, sometimes even by night, lighting up the whole city" (I.431). But he would have been a difficult member of an audience, "so carried away by his interest in singing and dancing that even at the public performances he could not refrain from singing with the tragic actor as he delivered his lines, or from openly imitating his gestures by way of praise or correction" (I.487).

Nero was even more theatrical: "He gave many entertainments of different kinds: . . . chariot races in the Circus, stage-plays, and a gladiatorial show" (II.103). He took extensive voice training, and "made his début at Naples, where he did not cease singing until he had finished the number which he had begun, even though the theater was shaken by a sudden earthquake shock" (II.115). Shortly afterward he was prevailed upon (tough task!) to sing in a public contest in Rome also: "He even thought of taking part in private performances among the professional actors. . ." (II.119). His youthful enthusiasm never waned:

> Toward the end of his life, in fact, he had publicly vowed that if he retained his power, he would at the games in celebration of his victory give a performance on the water-organ, the flute, and the bagpipes, and that on the last day he would appear as an actor and dance "Vergil's Turnus." Some even assert that he put the actor Paris to death as a dangerous rival. (II.183–85)

Such an exhibitionist would be apt to carry over his theatricality into his sex life, and Nero certainly did:

> He castrated the boy Sporus and actually tried to make a woman of him; and he married him with all the usual ceremonies, including a dowry and a bridal veil, took him to his house attended by a great throng, and treated him as his wife. . . . This Sporus, decked out with the finery of the empresses and riding in a litter, he took with him . . . at Rome through the Street of the Images, fondly kissing him from time to time.[15]

Nero's sexual imagination was wild, and he had the power to make his twisted fantasies come true:

> . . . he at last devised a kind a game, in which, covered with the skin of some wild animal, he was let loose from a cage and attacked the private parts of men and women, who were bound to stakes, and when he had sated his mad lust, was dispatched by his freedman Doryphorus; for he was even married to this man in the same way that he himself had married Sporus, going so far as to imitate the cries and lamentations of a maiden being deflowered. (II.133)

While Nero and Caligula were extreme cases, to be sure, their excesses tend to color our whole view of Imperial Rome. And even though they may not be representative of Roman patricians as a whole, they do embody the image of Rome which Volpone seems to have in his head.

2. "FOR ENTERTAINMENT OF THE GREAT VALOIS"

The Signiory of Venice never approached Nero's extravagance, but they certainly had elaborate festivities. Volpone mentions one of these in particular: the "entertainment of the great Valois" (3.7.161). I quote at length from an account of these festivities not so much because Jonson, the indefatigable researcher, probably read one or two of the many such narratives[16] as because this celebration is an especially good example of Venetian lavishness and display.

I quote extensively from Francesco Sansovino's *Venetia città nobilissima,* which Jonson may have seen because Lewkenor's excerpts from that work sent him to the original. Sansovino calls the celebrations for Henry III "the most elaborate welcoming ceremonies that were ever made by this state. . . ." The purpose was to show "how large the magnificence of the Venetian spirit is."[17]

Perhaps with an eye toward Henry's penchant for beautiful young men, the Signiory assigned forty young gentlemen to wait upon him during his stay, which lasted nine days. All forty met him, each in a separate decorated gondola. "Many pieces of artillery were fired, trumpets blown, drums beaten, and bells sounded"[18] as the Orators formally presented him with the young men.

A particularly sumptuous galley was built especially for the king, and Sansovino calls it "the most beautiful that ever came out of the Arsenal."[19] All around the boat were placed "thirty banners, some of white sarcenet, and blue, and some of red and yellow, with embroidery of gold and silver with lions of the Evangelist in the middle."[20] Ironic to us today, with our hatred of the institution of slavery, is this note: "And that which most gave to everyone marvelous delight were 354 slaves placed at the oars, all dressed in taffeta of yellow and peacock blue—the livery of this King."[21]

Before arriving at Venice itself, Henry was presented on the Lido with an elaborate triumphal arch in the Roman manner. It was designed by Palladio, and on the frontispiece were the usual effusive compliments in Latin. He was escorted to Venice by the Doge and Signiory in the ancient and exquisite ceremonial craft called the Bucentoro "with a perpetual thunder and booming of artillery, trumpets, drums, and bells, which went to the skies."[22]

Installed in the Foscari palazzo about midnight, the king "positioned himself at the window to see the marvelous spectacle of the multitude of boats . . . and the throng that remained on the banks at every point along the Grand Canal at windows and on roofs," in order to watch:

> But the most amazing thing of all was to see the infinite number of burning lights illuminate the night from one end of the canal to the other. They (the lights) were arranged diversely in the form of fleur-de-lis of France, pyramids, crowns, and various others . . . all the way from San Marco to Santa Lucia, a little less than two miles. And because all the lights reflected in the water with splendor, it appeared that under the Canal there was another starry sky, through which, all night long, went many gondolas filled with all sorts of people conversing at their leisure.[23]

Sansovino, with the kind of intense patriotism reserved for naturalized as opposed to native-born citizens,[24] concludes: "And it is not possible to make on earth a show more miraculous than this."[25]

A feast in the Grand Council chamber featured "two hundred gentlewomen of singular beauty, all dressed in white and adorned with pearls and with an infinite number of jewels of incredible value." These ladies danced elegantly, "stepping hand in hand in front of the King and bowing." For his part the King "stood always with hat in hand" as a sign of respect.[26] One table was loaded with "confections of sixty kinds, and with various statues and figures of sugar—of men, of nymphs, of lions, of ships, of griffons. . . ." Another had "three hundred figures of sugar, which were dispensed to the gentlewomen for favors."[27] Sansovino sums up with his usual hyperbole: ". . . the sight in that Great Chamber was similar to the Banquet of the Gods portrayed by the poets."[28]

Other authors of the time supplement the account of Sansovino. Some of these accounts are in Latin, which Jonson would presumably have found easier to read than Italian.[29] Vecellio's Latin text tells us that the king was stupefied by the pulchritude and magnificence of the two hundred ladies because not just head, neck, and breast, but sleeves and upper arms, were covered with gold and jewels and that "each one of the ornaments was judged to exceed the price of 50,000 pieces of gold."[30] Porcacchi compares Venice itself to a giant theater: he notes that the King placed himself so as ". . . to contemplate the magnificent and truly marvelous theater of the city of Venice."[31]

As for theater itself in Venice, it must be admitted that officially it was looked upon with suspicion:

> The government, after first of all prohibiting comedies in 1509, and then permitting them again, attempted, in 1518, 1521, and 1553, to put an end to scandals by fixing the hours, limiting the length of plays, forbidding representations at certain seasons and other provisions which were continually renewed, revoked, or violated.[32]

But along with this official suspicion was a private passion for theater: ". . . people . . . would climb walls, break open doors, or swim the canals to force their way into the place where some famous comedian was acting."[33] Sansovino tries to pretend that comedies were acted only at private feasts and during Carnival, but his defensive posture hardly conceals his enthusiasm for theater. He is lavish, for instance, in praise of Francesco Cherea, an actor who was a favorite of Pope Leo x.[34]

At the festivities for Henry III, the Signiory itself secured a famous Venetian *commedia* troupe to perform for the king:

> These Comedians the Gelosi, then, presented for the King a very agreeable and gracious tragicomedy, which he felt was marvelously pleasing. And I understand that they performed for him again Sunday evening, when they played a comedy, which the King showed that he enjoyed very much.[35]

In addition to *Commedia* troupes, there were in Venice from time to time theatrical productions by amateurs. The Company of the Calza, a social group, put on "comedies and other spectacles at very great expense."[36] That Coryat found the theaters inferior to those in London and added that Venetian actors cannot "compare with us for apparell, shewes and musicke" (I.386) does not say as much about the weakness of theater in Venice as it does about the strength of theater in London.

Venetian patricians, like the Roman emperors, had a reputation for indulging in illicit sex, though an infinitely less bizarre one. They had long had a reputation for sharing courtesans. In a novella Bandello tells the story of a prostitute ". . . who had ordinarily six or seven Venetian gentlemen as lovers."[37] Amelot de la Houssaye finds a bit of exhibitionism in this habit:

> . . . two, three, or four men to a Miss, and yet [they] agree very well: Nay that which in other places occasions Quarrels and Murder, is an indearment among them, and makes their intimacy the greater. In their Amours, they talk freely, and will discourse of their Alliances. . . . (p. 275)

II. Volpone as Eumolpus

In creating the character Volpone, Ben Jonson draws freely from the reputations of both Imperial Rome *and* Renaissance Venice, particularly as regards the three kinds of theatricality just reviewed. Let us turn to the play itself for evidence that Volpone does see himself, at least at times, as a character out of a first or second century satire—out of, say, Lucian, Horace, Juvenal, or Petronius.

Jonson uses Roman sources for the legacy-hunting plot. While legacy hunting doubtless existed in Renaissance Venice (as it has and does in most cultures, past or present), it does not seem to have been an *institution* in Venice in the same sense that it was in Imperial Rome.[38] In his introduction to the play C. H. Herford describes that sense well. He also tries to explain why Jonson chose the Venetian setting but does not question why the playwright—normally so scrupulous about accuracy of setting—should imagine a Roman institution in the midst of a Renaissance Venice in which the practice was not particularly widespread or noteworthy.[39]

Herford does, however, stress the importance of *The Satyricon* as a source. All editors note that both Petronius and Lucian create characters who bilk legacy hunters, but the characters in *Dialogues of the Dead* are mere sketches compared to Petronius's portrait of Eumolpus. Eumolpus is a major character throughout the entire last half of the lengthy narrative. An elderly poet, he is extremely intelligent and lives by his wits. This idea would appeal to Volpone, who is easily bored and cannot stand the tedium of his everyday identity of healthy magnifico.[40] The role of a decadent, penniless, adventurous con man would definitely have an attraction for him.

Eumolpus is shipwrecked near Croton, where he and

Encolpius (the narrator), and the others in their party are told that the town has a mania for legacy hunting:

> More astute than the rest of us, Eumolpus considered this new situation very carefully, declaring that such a method of getting rich did not at all displease him. . . . "I only wish," he said, "we could afford better scenery and props for the little comedy I have in mind."[41]

Petronius's language recognizes the essentially theatrical nature of the proposed con game—as does Jonson's in *Volpone* (Kernan's introduction to Yale ed., p. 10). Eumolpus continues: ". . . let's write the plot of our little play right now. Now if no one objects, I'll take the part of the master" (p. 127).

Eumolpus poses as a wealthy African landowner without heirs, the others as his servants. He coughs constantly and pretends to have diarrhea and a poor appetite. Volpone, too, pretends to have horrible diseases, including "my feigned cough" (1.2.124, 128 *s.d.*). Among the legacy hunters in Croton ". . . a great struggle broke out . . . to see which could shower Eumolpus with the most money" (p. 141). A lady legacy hunter offers her daughter and son, which is more depraved than Lady Would-be's offer of her own sexual favors and also more depraved than Corvino's offer of his wife. The lady's daughter, in great contrast to Celia, is quite willing to have "a lesson in ritual buttock-thumping" (p. 162). But Eumolpus has a problem: ". . . he had told everyone that he was gouty and cursed with a bad liver, and unless he maintained this fiction, he ran the risk of giving the whole show away" (p. 162). First he orders the girl to sit on his lap and "test for herself at close quarters the full extent of that 'uprightness and largesse and conspicuous humanity' her mother had just commended so warmly" (cf. Volpone telling Celia, and in some performances trying to show her, that he is "as fresh, / As hot, as high, and in as jovial a plight"—3.7.157–58—as he had been three decades earlier, when Henry III visited Venice). Here the novel and the play diverge, however: Eumolpus, by stationing a slave under the bed to push the mattress up and down, has a delightful time with the girl without betraying the fact that he is healthy. Volpone, by contrast, "gives the whole show away," though the damage is later temporarily repaired. It is a mystery why a character as brilliant as Volpone misses his estimate of Celia's morality so grossly. Perhaps he is so caught up in the role of Eumolpus that he cannot (for the moment) imagine that the girl in the story and Celia are utterly different.

In addition to Volpone's basic scheme, Jonson draws from the Roman satirists, historians, and moralists a good many incidental details. Much of the terminology, for instance, is more Roman than Venetian. Mosca is called Volpone's "parasite"; the phenomenon may be universal, but the term, as such, is Roman, not Venetian. Volpone's household "pets," Nano, Castrone, and Androgyno, were probably conceived by Jonson at least partly because of the habits of Nero and his ilk.[42] Venetians, in fact, had a reputation for being lavish in public but very frugal in their private households.[43] Volpone refers to the legacy hunters as "clients" (1.2.87), and J. D. Rea pointed out that the last three scenes of Act I are examples of a Roman "Salutatio," a custom that called for clients to visit their patron each morning,[44] a custom that does not seem to have been common in Venice. The beast fable element in the play is usually said to be mainly medieval in origin,[45] and perhaps it is; but legacy hunters are called vultures in Seneca and Martial, and Horace refers to one of them as the "gaping raven," an allusion to Aesop's fable of the fox and the cheese (cf. Volpone's comment about a fox "Mocking a gaping crow"—1.2.96).[46]

The Roman flavor of the play produced by the borrowings of plot and incidental details is increased by the borrowings in the dialogue itself, especially frequent in the speeches of Volpone and Mosca. I count nearly a score of such borrowings in the dialogue of each (even more in Mosca's if we include those from Lucian that are in the Pythagorean entertainment, which he wrote).[47]

Normally we attribute all these quotations and allusions to Jonson's own love of the classics. What I propose here is that we attribute the interest in things Roman to Volpone as a character. The best evidence for the proposal is to compare the allusions in the main plot to the allusions in the subplot. When Volpone and Mosca speak to each other, the dialogue is crammed with classical allusions; Sir Politic and Peregrine use scarcely any—instead, the dialogue is filled with Venetian local color. If Jonson were merely indulging his own interests without regard to characterization, we would expect the classical allusions to be distributed evenly throughout the play.

Volpone is by no means entirely lost in the past, however; he keeps at least one foot in the realities of the Venice of his own day. He is skilled at switching back and forth between one world and the other, and Mosca (probably to please his patron) is also. Two examples will serve to illustrate both their love for classical allusions and their facility at flip-flopping. Early in the play Mosca is praising Volpone's extravagance by quoting Horace's attack on miserliness:

> You are not like the thresher that doth stand
> With a huge flail, watching a heap of corn,
> And, hungry, dares not taste the smallest grain,
> But feeds on mallows and such bitter herbs.
> (1.1.53–56)

To this point Mosca is translating pretty closely. But then comes a divergence. Horace goes on to ridicule one who would "with a thousand jars—that's nothing, say three hundred thousand—of Chian and old Falernian stored in his cellars . . . drink sharp vinegar."[48] Mosca deftly substitutes the names of wines appropriate to modern Venice: "Nor like the merchant who hath filled his vaults / With *Romagnìa* and rich Candian wines, / Yet drinks the lees of Lombard's vinegar" (1.1.57–59). Mosca then goes right back to Horace, the next comparison ("You will not lie in straw whilst moths and worms / Feed on your sumptuous hangings"—1.1.60–61) being an almost literal translation.

In attempting to seduce Celia, Volpone first dangles before her "a rope of pearl, and each more orient / Than that the brave Egyptian queen caroused" (3.7.190–91), a reference to Cleopatra from Pliny. Then he offers "a carbuncle / May put out both the eyes of our St. Mark," an allusion which is clearly Venetian.[49] In the next line we are back with Pliny to "A diamond would have bought Lollia Paulina / When she came in like star-light, hid with jewels / That were the spoils of provinces" (194–96).

Allusions scattered throughout the main plot add even further to the Roman atmosphere. Volpone's *aubade* to his gold which opens the play is sprinkled with quotations from Pindar (probably by way of Lucian) and Euripides (probably by way of Seneca).[50] Since Volpone tells us that he glories more in the cunning purchase of his wealth than in the glad possession, Leggatt argues plausibly that the *aubade* is not the real Volpone speaking, that he is role playing.[51] I agree, and the role is that of pagan Roman. The nature of the freak show tells us much about Volpone's tastes. He likes travesty, but especially classical and learned travesty. Mosca knows his patron, and writes scripts accordingly.

Volpone acts Eumolpus convincingly ("I feel me going—uh!

uh! uh! uh!— / I am sailing to my port—uh! uh! uh! uh!—" 1.3.28–29) and then comments sagely on his fine results by quoting Seneca and Pliny (1.4.142–50). His role as Scoto of Mantua is quintessentially Venetian, of course, and he plays it well. But he reverts to the Roman role in his attempt to seduce Celia. It is here that we see in their most concentrated forms both his penchant for the classics and his obsessive theatricality. As audience, we love the theatrical moment when "*He* [Volpone] *leaps off from his couch*" (3.7.139, *s.d.*)—and so does he. His claim that he has visited her previously "in several shapes" (1.148) is a lie, since he discovered her existence only earlier that day; but the more disguises he can imagine himself donning, the better he likes it. He would like to rival the god Proteus himself in shape changing (11.150–53).

The ostensible point of his allusion to his acting in a comedy when Henry III visited Venice is that he is just as virile as he had been thirty years before; but the role he acted is of great interest here: Antinöus. A controversy has developed as to which of two classical figures of that name he represented. Herford and Simpson favored the beautiful young favorite of the Emperor Hadrian (IX.718). T. W. Craik, however, argued that the reference is to the chief suitor of Penelope in *The Odyssey.*[52] J. L. Simmons supports the latter view, noting that the allusion is probably to a specific *Ulysses Redux* acted at Oxford in 1592 in which Jonson would have had special reason to be interested.[53] Tay Fizdale suggests that Jonson was perhaps referring to both.[54] Craik reiterates his original position, whereas Douglas Brooks-Davies weighs in with good arguments on the Hadrianic side.[55] For my purposes here, however, it hardly matters whether Volpone was playing the decadent suitor, the decadent favorite, or both. In any case he is showing (a) that his fascination with acting goes back at least thirty years, and (b) that he likes classical roles, especially if he can represent someone decadent.

The rest of his seduction speech continues to show his obsessions with theatricality and with ancient Rome. Remembering the singing and dancing he did as Antinöus, he launches immediately into "Come, My Celia," with its well-known debt to Catullus. The parts of *Vivamus, mea Lesbia* which he imitates are notable for their *carpe diem* lyricism, but Catullus's reputation as one of the more obscene Roman poets is lurking not far in the background. The menu Volpone proposes for Celia (for example, "The heads of parrots, tongues of nightingales, / The brains of peacocks, and of ostriches"—3.7.201–02) is in imitation of one of the most decadent emperors of all, Heliogabalus.

Even the actual coupling of sex is imagined by Volpone as enhanced by a classical setting and by theatricality:

> Whilst we, in changed shapes, act Ovid's tales,
> Thou like Europa now and I like Jove,
> Then I like Mars and thou like Erycine;
> So of the rest, till we have quite run through
> And wearied all the fables of the gods.
> (3.7.220–24)

The easily wearied Volpone then imagines various modern costumes for her, including "one of our most artful courtesans"; but he moves fairly rapidly to an image that is probably from *The Satyricon:* ". . . transfuse our wand'ring souls / Out at our lips" and then back to Catullus again (11.236–39).

Volpone takes on another Venetian role, that of *commandatore,* and again acts it well—but the net result is disaster for his scheme. Rather than see Mosca the heir and married into the family of the Avocatore, the Fox uncases. He drops all roles and stands before the court as his true self—the healthy magnifico. This is the climactic moment in the play:

> I am Volpone, and this [*Indicating Mosca.*] is my knave;
> This [*Indicating Voltore.*] his own knave; this [*Indicating Corbaccio.*], avarice's fool; / This [*Indicating Corvino.*], a chimera of wittol, fool, and knave.
> And reverend fathers, since we all can hope
> Nought but a sentence, let's not now despair it.
> (5.7.89–93)

Though he has imitated others so much and so long that he is almost unable, when necessary for his essential dignity, to return to himself, he does finally come back: "I am Volpone." And that, I think, is one of the chief reasons that we have considerable sympathy for him. In the end, he rediscovers who he is.

III. The Crude Travelers: Lady Pol and Her Husband

To turn from Volpone to the Would-bes is to turn from a skillful

The habit of a commandatore. Volpone uses this very disguise in Act 5. The cap is even described in the text of the play; the angry Corvino berates the disguised Volpone about his "red, saucy cap, that seems to me / Nailed to your jolt-head with those two *chequins*" (*Volpone,* 5.8.16–17). He is clearly referring to the coin-like button or medallion pictured here. Presumably there is one just like it on the figure's unpictured side. From Cesare Vecellio, *De gli habiti antichi, et moderni* (Venice, 1590), Sig. P5. By permission of the British Library.

to two unskillful imitators. In *Discoveries* would-be poets get this advice:

> To make choise of one excellent man above the rest, and so to follow him, till he grow very *Hee:* or, so like him, as the Copie may be mistaken for the Principall. Not, as a Creature, that swallowes, what it takes in, crude, raw, or indigested. . . .[56]

Volpone does a convincing imitation of Eumolpus or, in any case, of a similar character from that culture and era; and the smoothness of his blend of classical quotations into dialogue shows that he has digested the Roman satirists. Sir Politic presumes to give advice to "your crude traveler" (4.1.7), by which he means an inexperienced one; but the digestive metaphor operates in that line just as it does in the quotation from *Discoveries.* Lady Pol and her husband devour all things Venetian, good or ill, and spit them back crude, raw, and indigested. The resulting humor is itself in some respects crude, but (to me, at any rate) quite funny.

Their lack of discrimination in what to imitate shows up most clearly in the Venetian figures whom the Would-bes choose as patterns. Both characters may be said to be trying to imitate two different models that are somewhat contradictory. Lady Politic is simultaneously trying to imitate a true lady out of Castiglione's *Courtier* (a book she mentions—4.2.35) and a Venetian courtesan, while Sir Pol is simultaneously trying to ape both a wise and sober Venetian statesman (cf. the image of Venice the Wise), and one of the notorious *bravi,* shady and dangerous intriguers—mostly foreign—who haunted the city.

1. LADY WOULD-BE ". . . AMONG THE COURTESANS"

Sir Politic claims that he and his wife are residing in Venice not primarily because *he* wants to but because *she* wants to: ". . . it is no salt desire / Of seeing countries . . . hath brought me out . . . But a peculiar humour of my wife's / Laid for this height of Venice, to observe, / To quote, to learn the language, and so forth" (2.1.5–6, 8, 11–13). Sir Pol discreetly fails to mention that she is in the city chiefly to imitate the fabled courtesans, but that idea seems to be common knowledge. Peregrine has just arrived, yet he has heard of her studies: "Your lady / Lies here in Venice for intelligence / Of tires, and fashions, and behaviour / Among the courtesans?" (2.1.26–29). Sir Pol admits so, and offers a feeble defense: "Yes, sir; the spider and the bee oft times / Suck from one flower." Lady Would-be considers the courtesans the flowers from whom she will suck the nectar of high fashion.

The courtesans were notorious for their high fashion, all right. Historical evidence on the point is abundant. Montaigne was amazed "to see so large a number of them (that is, courtesans), . . . spending money like princesses on dress and furniture, and yet having no other livelihood but that traffic" (*Diary*, p. 93). In addition to being expensive, their finery was immodest as well; like prostitutes of all ages they wanted to show as much skin as prevailing customs would allow. Even more than Venetian ladies, they painted their breasts. Vecellio says that they showed "not only their face but a great part of the breast—coated with white lead and painted."[57] Black-lace stockings are not entirely new, the courtesans having worn "see-through" embroidered stockings themselves. The courtesans use beauty aids, Vecellio says, such as cosmetics, various lotions, and bleaching of the hair.[58]

Coryat describes the fashions of the courtesans in exhaustive detail. Of cosmetics he reports:

> . . . thou maist easily discerne the effects of those famous apothecary drugs heretofore used amongst the Noble Ladies of Rome, even stibium, cerussa, and purpurissum. For few of the Cortezans are so much beholding to nature, but that they adulterate their faces. . . . (I.404)

Of hair style, this:

> . . . the silver tramels of her haire displayed in that curious manner besides her two frisled peakes standing up like prety Pyramides, that they give thee the true Cos amoris. (I.404)

Lady Politic tries hard to be a good student, but she has not mastered the arts. "This band," she complains, "Shows not my neck enough" (3.4.2–3). If she really wants to be seductive, she should realize that the competition is showing at least partial views of breasts and legs—the neck alone will never do. Her concern about the placement of her curl is accurate enough, as is her complaint about the fucus being too coarse (1.37). Her nose is red (3.4.16, 4.2.72–73), and that could certainly have been remedied by art.

But there is a more sinister sense in which she is attempting to imitate the courtesans: she is trying to trade sex for money. Her whole demeanor with Volpone in 3.4 is so flirtatious that we can scarcely doubt her willingness to barter with him directly, did she but know that he is healthy. As it is, she is forced to offer herself to Mosca instead:

> Remember what your ladyship offered me
> To put you in an heir; go to, think on't;
> And what you said e'en your best madams did
> For maintenance, and why not you?
> (5.3.40–43)

Her repeated urging to Peregrine that he "use" her is suspicious also: ". . . please you to use me, sir" (4.3.16) and again, "Pray you, sir, use me. In faith, / The more you see me, the more I shall conceive, / You have forgot our quarrel."[59]

Her wrath against Sir Pol's supposed "carnival concupiscence" (that is, his whore—4.2.60) is ironic because she herself is so libertine. She is surely one of those wives who, at Carnival time in Venice, help their gallants to get in the harvest of their amours. Likewise ironic is her accusation that the wench has fled to Venice for "liberty of conscience" (1.61). Parker's note accurately points out that the phrase usually meant "'freedom from religious persecution' (for which Venice was famous) but is being used ironically here, with 'liberty' implying 'licence'" (4.2.61n). One sixteenth-century travel writer uses the phrase with similar irony: Villamont. He asserts that in not a place in all Italy may one live in greater liberty than Venice, and the third and fourth reasons he gives in support of the idea are of special interest:

> . . . third, there is no Inquisition for one's faith at all; finally, each person lives there according to his fantasy and in liberty of conscience, which is why many French libertines live there—in order not to be sought out and controlled and in order to live there in all licence, along with great numbers from other nations, for the pleasure that they have each day.[60]

Sir Pol doubtless likes Venice's liberty of conscience in the religious sense, but his wife likes it in the sexual sense.

Lady Pol fails as a Would-be Courtesan not only because she lacks the requisite physical beauty (1.5.103–05) but also because she does not know when to shut up. Coryat praises the conversational abilities of the prostitutes:

> . . . thou wilt finde the Venetian Cortezan (if she be a selected woman indeede) a good Rhetorician, and a most elegant discourser, so that if she cannot move thee with all these foresaid delights, she will assay thy constancy with her Rhetoricall tongue. (I.405)

Lady Would-be considers herself a "most elegant discourser," all right, but, as Volpone moans in agony (in one of the funniest scenes in the play):

> All my house
> But now steamed like a bath with her thick breath.
> A lawyer could not have been heard; nor scarce
> Another woman, such a hail of words
> She has let fall.
>
> (3.5.7–11)

A few well-chosen words may heighten desire, but loquacity has just the opposite effect. A really accomplished courtesan would never make the mistake that Lady Would-be does.

As Creaser points out, in Lady Would-be's mind "courtly lady and courtesan are confused. . . ."[61] If Sir Pol's Bible is Contarini, Lady Would-be's is Castiglione's *Courtier.* Creaser's excellent note on the passage where she mentions this book (4.2.35) quotes relevant passages from Hoby's translation of Castiglione and indicates clearly how and why Lady Would-be fails to live up to the ideals set forth there.[62] I would add only that her reference to Aretino is hilariously inept. To call his pictures "a *little* obscene" (3.4.97—emphasis mine) is to engage in stupefying understatement.[63]

2. SIR POLITIC: "I KNEW THE FORMS . . . AND NOTHING ELSE"

John Chamberlain's admiration for Venetian statesmen is typical of those who subscribed to the positive side of the Myth. In a letter to Sir Ralph Winwood dated 15 February 1611, he describes the way Doge Leonardo Donato answered the English ambassador:

> . . . the Duke with a long and grave aunswer approving in a manner whatsoever he had saide. This duke is esteemed one of the most sufficient men of this age, and indeed yt is very rare and almost miraculous to see a man of his years (drawing toward fowrescore) of that dexteritie and pregnancie of wit and memorie, and withall

> of such redines of tongue and elocution, and I doubt whether theyre whole Senate (yf he were gon) could affoord them such another. . . .[64]

Sir Pol is clearly trying to imitate such men as the Doge. The English knight's opening line stresses wisdom, and is proverbial: "Sir, to a wise man all the world's his soil" (2.1.1). His initial caution in dealing with Peregrine is statesmanlike also. He inquires if the young man is traveling with license, a wise precaution. He carefully claims that he is not in Venice to practice Catholicism, and blames his wife for his presence in that city. Later, after he has gotten warmed up, he admits that he too has an interest in Venice:

> I do love
> To note and to observe; though I live out,
> Free from the active torrent, yet I'd mark
> The currents and passages of things
> For mine own private use, and know the ebbs
> And flows of state.
>
> (2.1.100–05)

Since Venice was very tolerant of foreigners' views as long as they did not preach them openly, the motives expressed here are entirely laudable and very much in accord with the sagacity Sir Pol is trying to ape.

Later we learn that Sir Pol has read "Contarine" (4.1.40). He could not have selected a better textbook to enable him to master the role of wise statesman in Venice. It contains a minute description of the complicated governmental machinery of Venice, enabling Sir Pol to chatter knowingly—albeit somewhat inaccurately—about the Great Council, the Forty, and the Ten.[65] Perhaps just as important for Sir Pol's purposes are the author's august reputation and the sagacious tone of the work. Contarini was one of the leading cardinals in certain Papal negotiations with the Lutherans, and a modern historian praises him for advocating a *via media* in these disputes.[66] The tone of *De Magistratibus* accords with the author's dignified career.

Almost up to the point of his final exit, Sir Pol is still valiantly attempting the Contarini role: to the disguised Peregrine he at first sends word that "he has weighty affairs of state / That now require him whole" (5.4.15–16).

Why does Sir Pol fail so miserably in his role as statesman?

One answer is Peregrine's—Sir Pol knows the outward forms of Venetian life, but nothing else. We can dig beneath that accurate statement. A good statesman is not credulous (we recall the suspicion—well-founded as it turns out—with which Shakespeare's Venetian Council in *Othello* greets the first reports that the Turk's main objective is Rhodes). Sir Pol believes all the reports of prodigies at home because he is deeply superstitious, feeling the need to throw three beans over his threshold when he discovers that a rat has "gnawn my spur leathers" (4.1.136–38). He also seems to believe the incredible claims of mountebanks. He believes, eventually, that Peregrine was indeed "A fugitive punk" (5.4.35);[67] and finally, to his utter downfall, he believes that the State of Venice is actually interested in arresting small fry such as he is who boast of plots "For discourse sake, merely" (5.4.47).

Another reason that Sir Pol fails as statesman is that he is attempting to play simultaneously certain aspects of another role: that of the *bravo.* The *bravi* were adventurers both from Venice and from other parts of Europe who were living by their wits and daggers in Venice. The type had achieved such notoriety by 1590 that Vecellio has a picture of the typical *bravo* costume. Coryat characterizes them as robbers and assassins (I.413), but the *bravi* were also known as intriguers and spies; and it is this bent of theirs that Sir Pol tries feebly to imitate. They are described by a modern historian as "men who haunted the piazza and gained a livelihood . . . by spying, by informations, and by murder."[68] Many were foreigners like Sir Pol: "Just as Venice became a resort of pleasure, so it provided a refuge for adventurers and social misfits from every part of Europe. And these made up the armies of the *bravi.*"[69] They formed a curious kind of fraternity:

> No one of these adventurers who arrived at Venice was likely to remain outside the floating population of his brothers whom he found already established there. His initiation would take no long time, and he would soon learn that under the life of the Venetians themselves there was a life of foreigners, *roués, declasssés*—men all of them engaged in intrigue of some sort. . . .[70]

The Signiory passed a strict decree banishing them all in 1600, but to no avail. Being mostly foreign, they would take refuge from arrest in their own embassies—and from that sanctuary mock the officers trying to arrest them. The Council of Ten, des-

A "bravo"—this distinctive kind of gentleman/spy/informer/ruffian may be relevant to an understanding of the character of Sir Politic Would-be in *Volpone.* From Cesare Vecellio, *De gli habiti antichi, et moderni* (Venice, 1590), Sig. X4 verso. By permission of the British Library.

perate, offered pardon to anyone who killed a *bravo,* which resulted in *bravi* murdering each other; but since many Venetian citizens were killing personal enemies and claiming that the dead men were *bravi,* this plan had to be abandoned.

Though nonviolent (to put it mildly), Sir Pol is just as fascinated with spying and intrigue as any *bravo.* He has been talking with Peregrine but a few minutes when he turns the conversation to espionage with the incredible theory that the whale in the Thames was actually a Spanish secret weapon and with the unbelievable claim that Stone the Fool was in secret a kind of James Bond. Peregrine tests him with even more unbelievable notions: that the baboons recently shown in London were spies and constitute "A kind of subtle nation near to China" (2.1.88–89). Sir Pol swallows this bait and swims blithely on, adding his own embellishments. As a "projector" (another current type), Sir Pol's commercial schemes are innocent enough (though the idea about herring is unpatriotic as favoring the Dutch over the English). His plan to cut down on quarantine delays is fanciful but harmless. It is the idea that he "could sell this state to the Turk" (4.1.130) that is dynamite. This remark is Sir Pol's most bravo-like boast because it is his boldest and most unprincipled. Even Venice's rivals among Christian powers gave lip-service to *La Serenissima*'s long struggle against the Turks. Sir Pol does not say that he *would* sell the State, of course, but even the boast that he *could* would raise some hackles, even among English audiences (cf. King James's "Lepanto," discussed earlier). Peregrine is not all that intelligent a character, since he genuinely believes that the encounter between him and Lady Would-be was entirely planned by Sir Pol; but the young man is bright enough to see that Sir Pol's careless remark about the Turks is a powerful weapon. Accordingly, he uses it in his elaborate practical joke in 5.4., and to devastating effect.

The *bravi* were also unprincipled (by sixteenth-century standards) as to religion, and Sir Pol advises the young traveler to imitate them in that:

> And then, for your religion, profess none,
> But wonder at the diversity of all;
> And, for your part, protest were there no other
> But simply the laws o' th'land, you could content you.
> Nick Machiavel and Monsieur Bodin both
> Were of this mind.
>
> (4.1.22–27)

Creaser points out how shallow the lumping together of these two great thinkers is,[71] but the point of interest here is that Venice was remarkable for the religious liberty allowed foreigners. To a strict Protestant like Ascham, this liberty was license; he thought that the kind of Erastianism recommended by Sir Pol was one of the chief traits of an Italianate Englishman, and that it was just a mask for atheism: "They make Christ and his gospel only serve civil policy; then neither religion cometh amiss to them; in time they be promoters of both openly, in place again mockers of both privily."[72]

Sir Pol is an even more abject failure as a *bravo* than he is as a statesman. Just as he cannot imitate the *Clarissimi* effectively because of his credulity, so he cannot imitate the *bravi* effectively because of his cowardice. Much of the comedy in his role arises, I think, from this trait. He makes only three appearances on stage, and each ends in flight. He flees the brawl precipitated when Corvino attacks Scoto/Volpone, credulously and egocentrically suspecting that it is "some trick of state" probably directed at him personally (2.3.10–12). He flees also when Lady Would-be attacks Peregrine, the supposed "female devil in a male outside" (4.2.56). He says to Peregrine, "Nay, / And you be such a one, I must bid *adieu* / To your delights. The case appears too liquid" (4.2.56–58). Finally, after the tortoise incident (5.4) he says that he will flee Venice itself.

Interestingly enough, however, Sir Politic does *not* say that he is going home. If he had said so, we could infer that he had been shocked out of his humour, had learned his lesson, and was returning to himself. Insofar as he has a real or ordinary self, it is that of English knight; and the only way he can return to himself is to return to England—in his case, geography is identity. The same is true of Lady Pol: ". . . she will straight to sea, for physic" (5.4.86). Venice has gotten rid of these two imitators of imitators, but neither says anything about returning home.

Indeed, Sir Pol can scarcely go home because he would have to endure there the taunts of the merchants, who seem to be English (note their mention of Fleet Street and Smithfield, 5.4.77–78). That Sir Pol must go "creeping with house on back" (5.4.88) is clearly a continuation of the tortoise imagery and also a final ironic comment on his first speech in the play: "Sir, to a wise man all the world's his soil."[73] Critics are right in seeing the Would-bes as parodies of Volpone,[74] but they have not given enough emphasis to one difference: Volpone returns to himself, the Would-bes do not. Such is the fate of Italianated English—trying to belong to two countries, in the end they belong to none.

* * *

Of the many helpful comparisons between *Volpone* and *Sejanus,*[75] few have focused on the uses of setting. No one would question the convincing quality of the setting in *Sejanus;* indeed, the more one reads in Tacitus and Suetonius, the more one admires Jonson's faithful and emotionally compelling portrayal of the Tiberian milieu. But Jonson gains a great deal in *Volpone* by shifting the scene from ancient Rome to Venice. He is able to use his intimate knowledge of Rome and yet to add a fascinating complexity by overlaying the ancient Roman setting with the Venetian one. Like Littlewit working over the Hero and Leander story, and yet with far happier results, he has taken *Sejanus* and ". . . made it . . . *moderne* for the times. . ." (*Bartholomew Fair* 5.3.120–21, H&S).

Conclusion: Shakespeare and Jonson Compared

If we look at the use of setting alone, the sharp contrast between Shakespeare and Jonson is clear. In both *The Merchant of Venice* and *Othello* Shakespeare begins his play in the city and later shifts the scene, creating rich comparisons and contrasts between Venice and Belmont, and Venice and Cyprus. Wholly different is Jonson's method. He insistently concentrates the action in Venice itself, not just to achieve unity of place but to give us, I would guess, an almost claustrophobic sense of urban density. As William Empson has remarked, "The arts are produced by overcrowding."[1] Shakespeare's method is more satisfying and more complex; but it is Jonson who creates a strong (and not entirely pleasant) sense of being *confined* to Venice, much as Volpone will be confined to prison and Mosca to the gallies.[2]

The similarities between the two playwrights in regard to their uses of the Myth of Venice have to do with characterization. In all three of the plays, certain leading characters are more easily understood against the background of the Myth of Venice. Antonio's sadness is more easily understood against a background of the decline of Venice as a merchant power; Bassanio's attempt to marry for money, against a background of the Venetian turn landward. The Myth also helps in understanding some relationships between characters: the declining social status of merchants and the growing popularity of aristocratic pursuits such as humanism and military science help to explain why Antonio perhaps feels a bit inferior to Bassanio, the scholar and soldier.

In *Othello,* too, the Myth helps us understand character. Iago's pornographic mind is more explicable seen against the Venetian reputation for condoning or even abetting the licentiousness of its young men. Othello had not one—but two—stereotypes working against him: both Moorish and Venetian husbands were thought to have been extremely prone to jealousy. Cassio's good-humored contempt for Bianca may be seen as related to the status of ordinary prostitutes in Venice. Desdemona's peculiar combination of boldness before the Council in 1.3 and her astounding naiveté about marital infidelity in 4.3 is less puzzling if we remember that both in fact and fiction an occasional Venetian daughter had good oratorical skills, and yet also remember that before their marriages they were watched even more warily than Venetian wives.

Even though Jonson does not deal in rounded characters as much as Shakespeare does, the Myth nevertheless helps us with character in *Volpone.* Volpone's passion for theatricality is more easily understood against the background of the extravagant theatricality prevalent both in ancient Rome and in Renaissance Venice, especially if we note that the rebirth was often said to have been that of the spirit of Rome transmigrating into Venice. Even the feeble and hilarious theatricality of the Would-bes is more explicable against the background of their unsuccessful attempts to imitate somewhat contradictory Venetian models.

Important as character is, the Myth aids in understanding at least one aspect of each play that is broader and more crucial than individual characters. Because the Venice of each play is a somewhat different Venice, we are pleased, but not surprised, to note that this larger aspect is quite different in the three plays.

In *The Merchant of Venice* the outstanding function of the Myth is to lend some credibility to two fairy-tale plots without, at the same time, destroying the atmosphere of romance. Venice was thought to be such an exotic place that the poet could give his characters a local habitation without reducing them to the plainness of the workaday world. In *Othello* the larger aspect is the sense of doom and inevitability felt by those in the audience who knew that Cyprus had long ago and forever fallen, and that the sexual reputation of Venice was such as to breed suspicion like the shambles breeds flies. In *Volpone* a heightened sense of the pervasive and excessive theatricality in both ancient Rome and its modern reincarnation, Venice, contributes to an understanding of the crucial thematic relationship in the play between theatricality and identity: one must know who one is, and the best way to lose that knowledge is to be constantly playing the role of someone else.

* * *

Trying to recover (by means of studies such as this one) what Peter Laslett calls "the world we have lost"[3] is an extremely difficult but also an extremely rewarding task. To use metaphors appropriate to Renaissance Venice, one hopes that this particular effort has unearthed the principal ways in which Englishmen at the turn of the seventeenth century viewed Venice and has used that treasure—hitherto partially buried—to purchase a better understanding of these three classic plays.

Abbreviations

EIC	*Essays in Criticism*
ELH	*English Literary History*
ELN	*English Language Notes*
ES	*English Studies*
JEGP	*Journal of English and Germanic Philology*
MLR	*Modern Language Review*
MP	*Modern Philology*
N&Q	*Notes and Queries*
PMLA	*Publications of the Modern Language Association*
RES	*Review of English Studies*
SEL	*Studies in English Literature*
ShS	*Shakespeare Studies*
SP	*Studies in Philology*
SQ	*Shakespeare Quarterly*
TSL	*Tennessee Studies in Literature*
TSLL	*Texas Studies in Language and Literature*
UTQ	*University of Toronto Quarterly*

Notes

Introduction: Urbs et Orbis

Sig. S2. Pighius is quoted by Franciscus Schottus, *Itinerarii Italiae* (Antwerp, 1600), Sig. A4v. The ultimate source of the wordplay is probably what Ovid said of Rome in *Fasti*, Loeb ed., trans. James G. Frazer (London: William Heinemann, 1931), Book II, line 684: "Romanae spatium est urbis et orbis idem."

1. For an account of all the plays before 1642 in which Venice is mentioned, see Edward Sugden, *A Topographical Dictionary to the Works of Shakespeare and His Fellow Dramatists* (London: Longmans, Green, 1925), *s.v.* "Venice."

2. For a good recent bibliography of work by historians on the Myth, see Margaret L. King, *Venetian Humanism in an Age of Patrician Dominance* (Princeton: Princeton University Press, 1986), p. 174n. See also Donald Queller, *The Venetian Patriciate: Reality vs. Myth* (Urbana: University of Illinois Press, 1986), pp. 3–28. A Dutch historian outlines the importance of the Myth in his native land, but admits that the effects were actually strongest in England; see Eco O. G. Haitsma Mulier, *The Myth of Venice and Dutch Republican Thought in the Seventeenth Century*, trans. Gerald T. Moran (Assen, The Netherlands: Van Gorcum, 1980), p. 54.

3. See Paster, *The Idea of the City in the Age of Shakespeare* (Athens: The University of Georgia Press, 1985). She makes several excellent points about Venice itself (see her index), but concentrates more on Rome and London. Earlier studies comparing *Othello* and *Volpone* on the basis of setting have also been helpful; see J. V. Crewe, "Death in Venice: A Study of *Othello* and *Volpone*," *University of Capetown Studies in English* 4 (1973): pp. 17–29; Brian Tyson, "Ben Jonson's Black Comedy: A Connection Between *Othello* and *Volpone*," *SQ* 29 (1978): pp. 60–66; Rosa Maria Colombo, "Venezia nel *Volpone* e nell'*Othello*," in *Shakespeare e Jonson: Il teatro elisabettiano oggi*, ed. Agostino Lombardo, Collana del Teatro di Roma 8 (Rome: Officina Edizioni, 1979), pp. 95–111.

4. On Shakespeare's knowledge of Latin, French, and Italian, see F. P. Wilson, "Shakespeare's Reading," *ShS* 3 (1950): p. 15; Kenneth Muir, *Shakespeare's Sources* (London: Methuen, 1957), pp. 1–7; Mario Praz, *The Flaming Heart* (1958; reprint, Gloucester, Mass.: Peter Smith, 1966), p. 164. No one would question Jonson's ability to read Latin, but his abilities in French and Italian have been doubted because of Drummond's sneer that Jonson did not "understand" either (*Conversations with Drummond*, in *Ben Jonson*, eds. C. H. Herford, Percy Simpson, and Evelyn Simpson [Oxford: Clarendon Press, 1925–52], I.134—hereafter abbreviated H&S). But "understand" may refer to the spoken language, and it is difficult to believe that someone with Jonson's abilities in Latin did not read simple French and Italian. (Although in a poem published in 1605 he admitted his inability to judge a translation from the French—see Epigram CXXXII in

H&S VIII. 83.) Modern scholars who have credited Jonson with knowing Italian include O. J. Campbell, "The Relation of *Epicoene* to Aretino's *Il marescalco,*" *PMLA* 46 (1931): p. 762; Daniel Boughner, *The Devil's Disciple: Ben Jonson's Debt to Machiavelli* (New York: Philosophical Library, 1968), p. 243; and Ian Donaldson, "*Volpone* 3.7.193–4 and *Il marescalco,*" *N&Q,* N.S. 29 (1982): pp. 139–40.

5. For instance, two of the best students of Shakespeare's use of Venice do not refer much to material in languages other than English: Nancy Elizabeth Hodge, "Shakespeare's Merchant and His Venice: Setting Antonio to Scale in His Proper World," diss., Vanderbilt University, 1984 and John W. Draper, *The* Othello *of Shakespeare's Audience* (1952; reprint, New York: Octagon, 1966). Jonson's possible resort to books in other tongues has been much better explored, especially by R. B. Parker in the introduction and notes to his Revels edition of *Volpone* (Manchester: Manchester University Press, 1983). All quotations of that play will be from this excellent edition unless otherwise specified, and will be cited parenthetically in the text (by act, scene, and line numbers).

6. Karl Elze, *Essays on Shakespeare,* trans. L. D. Schmitz (London, 1874), p. 272, 276, 294.

7. ". . . nicht Erzeugnis dichterischer Erfindung, sondern ein Spiegel der Wirklichkeit"—Theodore Elze, *Venezianische Skizzen* (Munich, 1899), p. 80.

8. Longer works on the subject tend to be general; see, for instance, Lewis Einstein, *The Italian Renaissance in England* (New York: Columbia University Press, 1902); Jeanette Fellheimer, "The Englishman's Conception of the Italian in the Age of Shakespeare," thesis, University of London, 1935; J. R. Hale, *England and the Italian Renaissance* (London: Faber and Faber, 1954); John Lievsay, *The Elizabethan Image of Italy.* Pub. for the Folger Shakespeare Library (Ithaca: Cornell University Press, 1964); Murray J. Levith, *Shakespeare's Italian Settings and Plays* (New York: St. Martin's Press, 1989). Levith, however, at least uses a geographical organization. (Chapter Two is specifically on Venice and the plays set there—pp. 12–39.)

9. Draper, for instance, charges that Shakespeare pictures Antonio in *Merchant* not as a magnifico but "as if he were a worshipful member of the Muscovy Company of London" (p. 18). More recently G. K. Hunter has argued that the Venice in Jonson's *Volpone* "is only a surface"—*Dramatic Identities and Cultural Tradition: Studies in Shakespeare and His Contemporaries* (Liverpool: Liverpool University Press, 1978), p. 23. More recently still Lars Engle refers often in his Marxist reading of *Merchant* to Lawrence Stone, *The Crisis of the Aristocracy, 1558–1641* (Oxford: Clarendon Press, 1965) but never to Venetian history; see "'Thrift is Blessing': Exchange and Explanation in *The Merchant of Venice,*" *SQ* 37 (1986): pp. 20–37. Levith argues frequently and specifically for the thinness of the disguise—see, for instance, the title of his first chapter, "Illyria, Italia, Englandia," and this passage from it: ". . . when we scratch the surface of Duke Orsino's Illyria in *Twelfth Night,* or indeed the surface of any of the Italian plays, we find Shakespeare's England" (Levith, *Shakespeare's Italian Settings and Plays,* p. 11).

I am not alone in questioning conventional wisdom on this point; see M. Berveiller, "Influencias italianas en las comedias de Ben Jonson," *Filosofia y letras* 3 (1942): p. 62: "El *Volpone* no es una trama londinense trapuesta a lengua veneciana" ("*Volpone* is not a London story transposed into Venetian language").

10. Among those who minimize the importance and accuracy of the Venetian background are William Matchett, "Shylock, Iago, and Sir Thomas More: With

Further Discussion of Shakespeare's Imagination," *PMLA* 92 (1977): p. 219; G. W. McWilliam, *Shakespeare's Italy Revisited* (Leicester: Leicester University Press, 1974), pp. 1–24. One small example: Gobbo's reference to his horse (*Merchant,* 2.2.95) has usually been seen as a slip by Shakespeare (what use horses in a city of canals?), but the historian Pompeo Molmenti has this note: "Nonetheless during the sixteenth century horses were to be seen in the city"–*Venice . . . From the Earliest Beginnings to the Fall of the Republic,* trans. Horatio F. Brown (London: John Murray, 1907; Chicago: A. C. McClurg, 1907), Part II, Vol. ii, p. 70 (cited hereafter in the following format: II.ii.70).

11. See, for instance, Robert Finlay, *Politics in Renaissance Venice* (London: Ernest Benn, 1980), p. 35.

Chapter 1. "I had read Contarine": Sources for Shakespeare and Jonson

1. Karl Elze, p. 262.
2. Ibid., p. 280.
3. Einstein, p. 370. Shakespeare's "fondness for Venetia" is indeed worth noting, however; under the dominion of Venice, and not all that far from it, were Padua *(Shrew)* and Verona *(Two Gentlemen, Romeo and Juliet).* With *Merchant* and *Othello* that makes five plays set in the area.
4. Henry Neville Maugham, *The Book of Italian Travel (1580–1900)* (London: Grant Richards, 1903), p. 15.
5. See Partridge, "Shakespeare and Italy," *English Studies in Africa* 4 (1961): p. 121; of the same period is Georges Lambin, *Voyages de Shakespeare en France et en Italie* (Geneva: E. Droz, 1962), pp. 10–11. Praz is firmly on the side of good sense: of the idea about the journey he says flatly that there is no evidence for it; see his article on Shakespeare and Italy in *A Reader's Encyclopedia of Shakespeare,* eds. Oscar James Campbell and Edward Quinn, (New York: Crowell, 1966), p. 393. Schoenbaum is more amiable and lenient, but still clearly throwing cold water: "A harmless fantasy to imagine Shakespeare enjoying an Italian holiday while in London the bell tolled for the dead. But most likely he stayed on in England."—*Shakespeare: A Documentary Life* (New York: Oxford University Press, 1975), p. 127.
6. *Calendar of State Papers, Venetian,* ed. Horatio F. Brown, Vol. 9 (1592–1603). Public Records Office (London: Her Majesty's Stationery Office, 1897), p. 79 (No. 184—17 July 1593) and p. 173 (No. 382—2 December 1595).
7. *The Correspondence of Sir Philip Sidney and Hubert Languet,* ed. and trans. Steuart A. Pears (London, 1845), pp. 8–10. The Earl of Derby was there in 1585; see Abel Lefranc, *A la découverte de Shakespeare* (Paris: Michel, 1950), II.356–80. The young Thomas Sackville, son of the Lord Treasurer, has been suggested as a possible oral source; see Theodore Elze, p. 29. One last example: Francis Russell, Second Earl of Bedford, was a notable Italianophile of the generation before Sidney; see Kenneth R. Bartlett, "The Strangeness of Strangers: English Impressions of Italy in the Sixteenth Century," *Quaderni d'italianistica* 1 (1980): pp. 57–58.
8. Logan Pearsall Smith, *The Life and Letters of Sir Henry Wotton,* 2 vols. (Oxford: Clarendon Press, 1907), I.48. Nathaniel returned to England in September 1606. Since *Volpone* was surely completed before March 25, any assistance procured by Jonson either directly or through John would have had to have

been by letters. John is generally believed to have been the "I.F." who wrote commendatory verses for the publication of the quarto of *Volpone* in 1607, though another possibility is John Florio.

9. George B. Parks, introduction to his ed. of William Thomas, *The History of Italy (1549)*, pub. for the Folger Shakespeare Library (Ithaca: Cornell University Press, 1963), pp. xvi-xvii. Subsequent references to Thomas will be included parenthetically in the text.

10. *The Rare . . . things which Edw. Webbe hath seene . . . in the Gallies . . . of the great Turke* (London, 1590), Sig. C4.

11. Stoye, *English Travellers Abroad, 1604–1667: Their Influence in English Society and Politics* (London: Jonathan Cape, 1952), p. 118.

12. H&S, I. 40–41, 202.

13. Hodge diss., pp. 16–17; Sergio Rossi, "Note sugli Italiani in Inghilterra nell'età del Rinascimento" in *Saggi sul Rinascimento,* ed. Rossi, Biblioteca di Anglistica: Collano di testi e studi, Vol. I (Milan: Edizioni Unicolpi, 1984), pp. 55–115; and Giuseppe S. Gargano, *Scapigliatura italiana a Londra sotto Elisabetta e Giacomo I°* (Florence: L. Battistelli, 1923).

14. *The Travels and Life of Sir Thomas Hoby . . . Written by Himself. 1547–1564,* ed. Edgar Powell. Camden Miscellany, x, Part 2. Camden Third Series, IV (London: Royal Historical Society, 1902). Subsequent references will be included parenthetically in the text.

15. Fox, Servant to Henry Cavendish, *Mr. Harrie Cavendish His Journey to and from Constantynople, 1589,* ed. A. C. Wood. Camden Miscellany, XVII, Part 2. Camden Third Series, LXIV (London: Royal Historical Society, 1940), pp. 12–13.

16. Fynes Moryson, *An Itinerary Containing His Ten Yeares Travell . . .* (Glasgow: James MacLehose, 1907), I.158–196. Subsequent references will be included parenthetically in the text.

17. Frances Yates doubts whether Florio had ever been to Venice; see *John Florio* (Cambridge: Cambridge University Press, 1934), p. 21. Lewkenor admits in his preface that he has never been there; see *The Commonwealth . . . of Venice* (1599), Sig. A2. Subsequent references to Lewkenor will be included parenthetically in the text.

18. On Florio and Shakespeare, see Clara Longworth de Pineton, Countess of Chambrun, *Giovanni Florio: Un Apôtre de la Renaissance en Angleterre à l'époque de Shakespeare* (Paris: Payot, 1921), p. 134; Frances Yates, *Florio,* pp. 334–36; Praz, *Encyclopedia,* ed. Campbell, p. 393. On Jonson and Florio, see Piero Rébora, *L'Italia nel dramma inglese* (Milan: "Modernissima," 1925), p. 118 and Praz, "Ben Jonson's Italy" in *The Flaming Heart,* pp. 176–81.

19. H&S, I, facing p. 56. We should not, however, think of Florio as Jonson's *only* source, as Mario Praz seems to do (*The Flaming Heart,* p. 166). Besides the probability that Florio had never been to Venice, his list of works consulted in compiling his dictionary does not contain any guidebooks. I am convinced that while Jonson drew his Italian vocabulary from Florio, he drew his Venetian local color largely from other sources.

20. See Yates, *A Study of Love's Labour's Lost* (Cambridge: Cambridge University Press, 1936), pp. 20–49.

21. See Kenneth Muir, "Shakespeare and Lewkenor," *RES* 7 (1956): pp. 182–83 and Daniel Boughner, "Lewkenor and *Volpone, N&Q,* N.S.9 (1962): pp. 124–30.

22. Whitfield, "Sir Lewis Lewkenor and *The Merchant of Venice:* A Suggested Connexion," *N&Q,* N.S. 11 (1964): pp. 123–33.

23. *The Resolved Gentleman,* a translation (via Spanish) of the French of Olivier de La Marche's *Le Chevalier delibéré* (London, 1594) and *The Estate of English Fugitives under the King of Spain* (London, 1595).

24. David McPherson, *Ben Jonson's Library and Marginalia, SP,* Texts and Studies Issue, 71 (1974): p. 48.

25. On that favorable view, see Zera S. Fink, *The Classical Republicans: An Essay in the Recovery of a Pattern of Thought in Seventeenth Century England.* Northwestern University Studies in the Humanities, No. 9 (Evanston: Northwestern University Press, 1945), Chapter 1; J. G. A. Pocock, *The Machiavellian Moment: Florentine Political Thought and the Atlantic Republican Tradition* (Princeton: Princeton University Press, 1975), pp. 272–330.

26. Geoffrey Bullough, *Narrative and Dramatic Sources of Shakespeare,* 7 vols. (London: Routledge, 1973), VII, pp. 262–65; Emrys Jones, "Othello, 'Lepanto' and the Cyprus Wars," *ShS* 21 (1968): pp. 47–52.

27. On Holofernes and the proverb, see Chapter 2. For a complete list of language books see R. C. Simonini, Jr., "Italian-English Language Books of the Renaissance," *Romanic Review* 42 (1951): pp. 241–44.

28. William Painter, *The Palace of Pleasure* (1566, 1575), ed. Joseph Jacobs, Fourth ed. (London, 1890) and Matteo Bandello, *Tragical Tales,* trans. Geoffrey Fenton (Anno 1567), ed. Hugh Harris. Broadway Translations (London: Routledge, 1924).

29. These books, especially the later versions, are more than translations of Botero. Johnson has added material from various other sources. The first edition does not contain anything on Venice, but the other two do.

30. Guylforde, *Pylgrymage . . . to the Holy Land,* A.D. *1506,* ed. Sir Henry Ellis (London, 1851) and Boorde, *The First Boke of the Introduction of Knowledge (1542),* ed. F. J. Furnivall (London, 1870). Guylforde will hereafter be cited parenthetically in the text.

31. The original Latin is an epistle to the young nobleman Philip Lanoy; see Lipsius, *Epistolarum Centuriae Duae* (Frankfurt, 1591), Centuria I, Epist. xxii, Sigs. C4–C7v.

32. Boughner makes this point, p. 124.

33. For instance, in the Venice ed. of 1591, Contarini's text (in Italian) ends on Sig. G6 and Giannotti's begins, Sig. G6v.

34. For a biography and liberal excerpts in English, see Patricia Labalme, *Bernardo Giustiniani: A Venetian of the Quattrocento* (Rome: Edizioni di storie e letteratura, 1969).

35. I have used Münster, *Cosmographiae Universalia Lib.* VI (Basel, 1550).

36. Sansovino, *Delle cose notabili della città di Venetia* (Venice, 1587). Subsequent references, all to this edition unless otherwise specified, will be included parenthetically in the text. On the authorship question, see Note 21 of my article, "Lewkenor's Venice and Its Sources," *Renaissance Quarterly* 42 (1988): p. 464.

37. These details make the book valuable to art historians even today, so much so that a later edition (1663) has been reprinted in facsimile, ed. Jennifer J. Fletcher (Farnborough, Hants.: Gregg Intl., 1968). I have consulted the 1581 and 1604 editions as well as this facsimile. Subsequent references will be to the 1667 edition unless otherwise indicated, and all references (regardless of edition) will be included parenthetically in the text.

38. Boughner argues that in *Sejanus* Jonson is indebted to Machiavelli's *Discourses;* see *Devil's Disciple,* p. 243. Bodin's *République* was first published in French (Paris, 1576); see also the Latin *De Republica* (Lyon, 1586 and Frankfurt,

1591) and the English (too late unless consulted in manuscript), trans. Knolles (1606). Bembo's history of Venice covering the years 1487–1513 was first published in Latin (Venice, 1551); I have used the Italian translation, *Della historia Vinitiana [sic]*, trans. and updated by Alemanio Fino (Venice, 1570).

39. See Botero, *The Reason of State*, trans. P. J. and D. P. Waley and *The Greatness of Cities*, trans. Robert Peterson (London: Routledge, 1956). Botero's *Relatione della republica Venetiana* (Venice, 1605) was probably too late for even Jonson to have used, but is interesting.

40. In Bandello, for instance, the following stories are set in Venice and contain a few bits of local color: I.xv, xxxv; II.iv, xli; III.iv, xxiii, xxxi. See *Tutte le Opere*, ed. Francesco Flora (Milan: Mondadori, 1934–1935).

41. The earliest edition of Alberti that I have found reference to is Bologna, 1550, but it was also reprinted in Venice, 1553, 1557, 1561, etc. It also appeared in Latin (Cologne, 1567). Inigo Jones owned a copy of the 1588 Venice edition in Italian; see J. Alfred Gotch, *Inigo Jones* (London: Methuen, 1928), p. 252.

42. Pighius, tutor to the promising young son of the Duke of Cleves, accompanied his pupil on an educational journey to Italy, where the prince suddenly died. *Hercules Prodicius* (Antwerp, 1587) is both a panegyric of the prince and an account of their journey.

43. I have used *Les Voyages du Seigneur de Villamont* (Arras, 1598). E. S. Bates says that Villamont was the book of European travel most frequently reprinted in Shakespeare's lifetime; see *Touring in 1600: A Study in the Development of Travel as a Means of Education* (Boston: Houghton Mifflin, 1911), p. 87.

44. Zaltieri's (BM Pressmark C.7.e.2, Map No. 66) is dated (on the map itself) 1566. Braun and Hogenberg's *Civitates Orbis Terrarum* (Cologne, 1572–1598) reprints Zaltieri. The collection was itself reprinted (Cleveland: World Publishing Co., 1966). See I.505.

45. Vecellio, *De gli habiti antichi, et moderni di diverse parti del mundo* (Venice, 1590, 1598). Subsequent references will be included parenthetically in the text.

46. Other costume books printed closer to London contain some pictures of Venetian types, but not anything like so many as are in Vecellio's; and there is nothing resembling Vecellio's extensive commentary. See, nevertheless, Abraham de Bruyn, *Omnium . . . Gentium Habitus* (Antwerp, 1581); Jean Jacques Boissard, *Habitus Variarum Orbis Gentium* (Mechlin, 1581); Hans Weigel, *Habitus Praecipuorum Populorum* (Nuremberg, 1577).

Chapter 2. Venetia, Venetia: The Myth of Venice

1. Q and F print *Vemchie vencha, que non le unde, que no te perreche.* I quote the corrected version from the Riverside edition, ed. G. Blakemore Evans *et al.* (Boston: Houghton Mifflin, 1974). All subsequent quotations of Shakespeare will also be from this ed. (unless otherwise indicated), and will be cited parenthetically in the text (by act, scene, and line numbers).

2. This is the version in Florio's *Second Fruites* (1591), Sig. Pv, P2.

3. "Possiamo parlare d'un mito di Venezia-stato-misto, d'un mito di Venezia-stato-di-libertà, d'un mito di Venezia-città-galante"—Franco Gaeta, "Alcuni considerazioni sul mito di Venezia," *Bibliothèque d'humanisme et Renaissance* 23 (1961): p. 60.

4. Gaeta, p. 75.

5. Logan, *Culture and Society in Venice, 1470–1740* (London: B. T. Batsford, 1972), p. 13.

6. E.g., Pullan, *Rich and Poor in Renaissance Venice* (Oxford: Basil Blackwell, 1971).

7. Justus Lipsius, *A Direction for Travailors*, trans. J. Stradling (1592), Sig. D. See also *Second Fruites*, Sig. P2, P3.

8. ". . . la città la più copiosa, & la più ricca che sia sotto il cielo"—Francesco Sansovino, *Ritratto della più nobili et famose città d'Italia* (Venice, 1575), Sig. Ii2v.

9. ". . . un Paradiso terreno"—Sansovino, *Delle cose notabili*, 1587, Sig. E7.

10. *Canon Pietro Casola's Pilgrimage to Jerusalem in the Year 1494*, ed. and trans. M. Margaret Newett (Manchester: Manchester University Press, 1907), p. 125. Subsequent references will be included parenthetically in the text.

11. *Itinerary* (1600), trans. Edmond Warcupp (1660), p. 11 and *Volpone* 3.7.192–93. Other references to the Treasury and the carbuncle include the following: Sansovino, *Venetia*, 1581, Sig. k2v; Comines, trans. Danett (1596), Sig. Dd3v; Thomas, ed. Parks, pp. 75–76; Thomas Coryat, *Crudities*, 1611 (Glasgow: James MacLehose, 1905), I. 356; Moryson, I.171–72. Subsequent references to Coryat will be included parenthetically in the text.

12. *Politick Discourses*, 1599, trans. Henry [Carey], Earl of Monmouth (1657), p. 118. Subsequent references will be included parenthetically in the text.

13. William H. McNeill, *Venice: The Hinge of Europe, 1081–1797* (Chicago: University of Chicago Press, 1974), p. 22.

14. Bates, p. 104.

15. Ibid., pp. 104–5.

16. On the explosion see Sansovino 1581, Sig. Xxx3; *Delle cose notabili*, 1587, Sig. F; Lewkenor, Sig. Gg4; see also *Volpone* 4.1.85–99.

17. "Vi si vede in questa città infinito numero d'huomini di diverse parti del mondo, con diversi habiti, per traficare, mercantare; & veramente è cosa maravigliosa à veder tanta diversità di persone, vestiti di diversi habiti"—Alberti, 1577, Sig. Kv.

18. ". . . frequentati da i mercanti Fiorentini, Genovesi, Milanesi, Spagnuoli, Turchi, & d'altri nationi diverse del mondo"—Sansovino, *Venetia*, 1581, Sig. L12.

19. See Franco, *Habiti d'huomeni [sic] et donne Venetiane* (Venice, ca. 1609), Fol. 28 and Parker's edition of *Volpone*, Plate 4.

20. ". . . si vous estes curieux de voir des hommes de toutes les parties du monde, vestus chacun à sa mode diversement, allez à la place de S. Marc, ou celle de Rialto, ou vous trouverez toutes sortes de personnes"—Villamont 1598, Sig. N6.

21. "In summa, urbs illa magnificentissima, pulcherrima & ditissima, facta est regina maris, habitaturque à maxima frequentia populi, ex diversis nationibus, imò ex toto fermè orbe ad exercendam mercaturam illic concurrentis"—*Cosmographiae* 1550, Sig. o2.

22. See, for instance, Frederick C. Lane, *Venice: A Maritime Republic* (Baltimore: Johns Hopkins University Press, 1973), pp. 292–94; Brian Pullan, introduction to Alberto Tenenti, *Piracy and the Decline of Venice, 1580–1615*, trans. Janet and Brian Pullan (London: Longman's, 1967), p. xii; Oliver Logan, *Culture and Society*, p. 24. McNeill points out (p. 143) that the all-time high for anchorage taxes was 1603–1605 and for woolen cloth production, 1602.

23. ". . . the Portugals . . . found out the voyaging into the *Indies*, to the exceeding prejudice of *Venice*, who before had thence al their spices, with which

in a manner they furnished all the western provinces of Christendome"—Lewkenor, Sig. Gg2v.

24. DuBellay, *Les Regrets*, Sonnet 125 in Beatrix Ravà, *Venise dans la littérature française depuis les origines jusqu'à la mort de Henry IV* (Paris: Edoard Champion, 1916), p. 389.

25. See the second of two 1599 editions, Sig. A4v.

26, Boccalini, *I Ragguagli di Parnasso: or Advertisements from Parnassus*, trans. Henry [Carey], Earl of Monmouth (London, 1656), p. 254. Subsequent references will be included parenthetically in the text.

27. "Car les loix des hommes sages & prudents sont l'ame de la republique"—Villamont 1598, Sig. M6v.

28. *The Estates, Empires, & Principallities of the World*, trans. Edward Grimestone (London, 1614), Sig. Yy6. Subsequent references will be included parenthetically in the text.

29. *The History of Venice*, 1605, trans. Henry [Carey], Earl of Monmouth (London, 1658), p. 2.

30. M. F. Mallet and J. R. Hale, *The Military Organization of a Renaissance State: Venice c. 1400 to 1617* (Cambridge: Cambridge University Press, 1984), p. 314.

31. Howell, *S.PQ.V. A Survay of the Signiorie of Venice* (1651), Sig. C2ff. Subsequent references will be included parenthetically in the text.

32. Tommasso Porcacchi, *Le attioni d'Arrigo Terzo Rè di Francia . . .* (Venice, 1574), Sig. E4v–F. I say Jonson might have come across it because it is one of the few pamphlets among the many that describe Henry III's visit to Venice which specifically mentions the *comedies* with which he was entertained (cf. "At recitation of our comedy / For entertainment of the great Valois"—*Volpone* 3.7.160–61). Other instances of the Venice-as-Virgin metaphor include Botero, *An Historicall Description*, 1603, Sig. Q3v; Coryat, 1905 ed., I.301. For a fuller discussion of the history of the metaphor, see Milton Wilson, "Travellers' Venice: Some Images for Byron and Shelley," *UTQ* 43 (1974): pp. 102–4.

33. Wordsworth, *Complete Poetical Works*, Cambridge ed. (Boston: Houghton Mifflin, 1932), pp. 285–86.

34. "Ma nell'historia Venetiana si vede il contrario . . . si dice, che i Venetiani hanno fatto questa cosa, e quella, non il tale, o il tale"—Botero, *Relatione della republica Venetiana* (Venice, 1605), Sig. M4.

35. See 2.1.119–20. Molmenti oversimplifies, but the observation is interesting.

36. McNeill, p. 23. Other recent historians, however, have been exposing cracks in the facade of Venetian unity; see Charles J. Rose, "Marc *[sic]* Antonio Venier, Renier Zeno and 'The Myth of Venice,'" *The Historian* 36 (1974): pp. 479–97.

37. Abraham Nicholas Amelot de la Houssaye, *The History of the Government of Venice*, trans. anonymous (London, 1677), p. 286. Subsequent references will be included parenthetically in the text.

38. Bodin, *Republic*, ed. Kenneth Douglas McRae. Harvard Political Classics (Cambridge: Harvard University Press, 1962), p. 711. Subsequent references will be included parenthetically in the text.

39. Moryson, *Shakespeare's Europe*, ed. Charles Hughes (1903; rpt. New York: B. Blom, 1967), p. 139.

40. Quoted in John R. Hale, ed. *Renaissance Venice* (London: Faber and Faber, 1973), p. 455.

41. La Boetie, *Anti-Dictator,* trans. Harry Kurz (New York: Columbia University Press, 1942), p. 21; Vettori quoted in Finlay, p. 36.
42. Michel de Montaigne, *The Diary of Montaigne's Journey to Italy in 1580 and 1581,* trans. E. J. Trechmann (London: Leonard and Virginia Woolf, 1929), p. 91. Subsequent references will be included parenthetically in the text.
43. Misson in *Navigantium atque Itinerantium Biblioteca,* ed. John Harris (London, 1705), II.656–57; Alexandre Toussaint Limojon de Saint Didier, *The City and Republick of Venice,* trans. Fra Terne [a pseudonym] (London, 1699), Part 2, pp. 122–23. (*BM Cat.* indexes under LIMOJON.) Both Misson and Saint Didier will hereafter be cited parenthetically in the text.
44. Samuel Lewkenor, *A Discourse of . . . Citties wherein doe flourish . . . priviledged Universities* (1600), Sig. I2.
45. Labalme, p. 284.
46. Finlay, p. 33.
47. Molmenti, II.i.230.
48. Lithgow, *The Total Discourse of the Rare Adventures and Painefull Peregrinations* (Glasgow: James MacLehose, 1906 [based on 1632 ed.]), pp. 33–34.
49. *Shakespeare's Europe,* pp. 164–65.
50. Molmenti, II.i. 30, 37.
51. *Ye Oldest Diarie of Englysshe Travell: Sir Richard Torkington . . . 1517,* ed. W. J. Loftie (London, c. 1880), p. 7.
52. Montaigne's lodgings were unsatisfactory, but he did not move because he was not planning to stay in the city very long anyway (*Diary,* p. 250). Languet wrote to Sidney, "I judge from your letter that the splendour of Venice does not equal your expectation" (*Correspondence,* p. 12).
53. Lassels, *The Voyage to Italy* (Paris, 1670), p. 426.
54. Molmenti, II.i. 73.
55. Muir, *Civic Ritual in Renaissance Venice* (Princeton: Princeton University Press, 1981).
56. "Et il Fontico de i Tedeschi costumava ne i tre giorni avanti a quello di Carnovale, di far festa publica a porte aperte. Dove concorrevano tutte le mascare di quel tempo, in un perpetuo ballo, che durava per i predetti tre giorni. Si fecero etiandio bellissime & ricchissime mascarate, con diverse livree di cavalli, con corsi di tori, & con giostre di lancie, & con diverse musiche. . ."—Sansovino 1581, Sig. Tt4v.
57. Molmenti, II.i. 76n.
58. "Et le donne mettendosi intorno intorno alla piazza su per le finestre, aspettano la ricca pompa che dee venire"—*Delle cose notabili* 1587, Sig. E5v.
59. These are listed in the notes to Chapter 5.
60. Denis Arnold, "Venice" in *The New Grove Dictionary of Music and Musicians,* ed. Stanley Sadie (London: Macmillan Co., 1980), Vol. 19, p. 614–17.
61. Molmenti, II.i. 263.
62. Coryat, I. 402; Molmenti, II.ii. 241; Sanudo quoted by Molmenti; Fox, p. 13.
63. "Ma non si può già facilmente descrivere, come elle s'acconcino la testa, nè si veggono alle finestre, frequentando elle più tosto la porta, & la strada, per tirar nella ragna gli uccellacci, che passano. Quivi si trattengono cantando canzonette amorose, ma con poca gratia, & conforme alla lor vile conditione, facendosi di più quasi tutte sentir con la voce roca"—Vecellio 1590, Sig. T2v.
64. See *Delle cose,* Sig. B4–B4v and Saint Didier, Part 3, p. 48.

65. Paolo Giovio speaks of the Venetians having "incredibile desiderio di conservare la libertà"; see *Delle istorie del suo tempo* (Venice, 1565), Sig. A3v. The terms of my exposition are from Pullan, *Rich and Poor,* p. 4.

66. "Many gentlemen and others who seek only their ease, and to live without care, retire to Venice as much to be in liberty as to court women there." (". . . plusieurs Gentilshommes & autres qui ne cherchent que leur aise, & vivre sans grand soucy, se retirent à Venise, tant pour y estre en liberté, que pour y courtiser les Dames")—*Le Seconde tome des histoires tragiques, extraites de l'Italien de Bandel . . . par Françoys de Belleforest* (Paris, 1565), p. 276.

67. ". . . sunt quidem forma bona sed gestus, & mores, planè meretricios habent. . . ."—Philalethes, Polytoipiensi [pseud. Lando], *Forcianae Quaestiones* [Naples, 1536], Sig. B5.

68. Estienne, *Deux dialogues du nouveau langage françois italianizé,* ed. Isidore Liseux (Paris, 1883), I.228.

69. "Mais les Romaines, Milannoises, Neapolitaines, Florentines, Feraroises, & autre Dames d'Italie sont beaucoup plus modestes pour ce regard, car . . . ne descouvrent elles leurs tetins"—Villamont, 1598 ed., Sig. N8v.

70. John Ray in *Navigantium,* ed. Harris, II.561, Col. 1.

71. William Bousma, "Venice and the Political Education of Europe" in Hale, ed., *Renaissance Venice,* p. 461.

72. Hale, ed., *England,* p. 30.

73. McPherson, "Lewkenor's Venice," p. 461.

74. Einstein, p. 121n, who cites Archivio Mediceo, Florence, 4185.

75. James Howell, *Instructions for Foreign Travel* (1642), Sig. F4 (p. 105).

76. *A Most Delectable, and True Discourse, of an admired and painefull peregrination. . .* (1614), Sig. C3v.

77. Einstein, p. 121.

78. Smith, I. 317.

79. Molmenti, II.i. 23n. See also John Lievsay, *Venetian Phoenix: Paolo Sarpi* (Lawrence: University of Kansas Press, 1973). For a notable attack on Venetian secularism by a Cinquecento Pope, see *Memoirs of a Renaissance Pope: The Commentaries of Pius II: An Abridgement,* trans. Florence A. Gragg, ed. Leona C. Gabel (London: Geo. Allen and Unwin, 1960), pp. 301–06.

Chapter 3. *The Merchant of Venice* and the Myth

1. Previous studies of the Venetian background of this play include the following: the Hodge dissertation, already cited (which is fullest and best); Cary F. Jacob, "Reality and *The Merchant of Venice,*" *Quarterly Journal of Speech* 28 (1942): pp. 307–15; John W. Draper, "Shakespeare and the Doge of Venice," *JEGP* 46 (1947): pp. 75–81; Brian Pullan, "Shakespeare's Venice," *Listener* 89 (18 January 1973): pp. 79–82; McWilliam, *Shakespeare's Italy,* pp. 1–24; Hunter, *Dramatic Identities,* pp. 23–24, 26–28; Walter Cohen, "*The Merchant of Venice* and the Possibilities of Historical Criticism," *ELH* 49, no. 4 (1982): pp. 765–89; Cecil Roth, "The Background of Shylock," *RES* 9 (1933): pp. 148–56 and *History of the Jews in Venice* (1930; reprint, New York: Schocken, 1975).

2. "Mine argosy from Alexandria / Loaden with spice and silks. . ."—ed. Richard Van Fossen (Lincoln: University of Nebraska Press, 1964), 1.1.44–45.

3. Pullan, *Listener,* p. 80.

4. *Historie of Italie,* Sig. EE2v.

5. Shakespeare's main source was, of course, Ser Giovanni Fiorentino, *Il pecorone* (Milano, 1558), Giornata Quarta. Because of the convenience of the Italian and English printed together, I have used for the source *Shakespeare's Library*, ed. W. C. Hazlitt, 2nd ed., rev., 6 vols. (ca. 1875; reprint, New York: AMS Press, 1965), Section 1, Vol. 1, pp. 319–53.

6. Lawrence Danson, *The Harmonies of* The Merchant of Venice (New Haven: Yale University Press, 1978), pp. 19–55. I am not alone in challenging Danson's view. In doing so I follow Engle, "'Thrift is Blessing,'" 21–22. Earlier attempts to explain the melancholy include Graham Midgley, "*The Merchant of Venice:* A Reconsideration," *EIC* 10 (1960): pp. 119–33; John D. Hurrell, "Love and Friendship in *The Merchant of Venice,*" *TSLL* 3 (1961): pp. 328–41; Fernando Ferrara, "La commedia e la vita" in *Shakespeare e la commedia* (Bari: Adriatica Editrice, 1964), pp. 276–85.

7. As early as 1605, we get this heading in Botero's *Relatione:* "Se l'haver atteso alla terra firma sia stato utile à Venetiani, or nò" (Sig. A3v). Paruta, however, in 1599, defended the turn landward as a wise move; see *Politick Discourses* (1657), p. 115.

8. Memmo, *Dialogo . . . nel quale dopo alcune filosofiche dispute, si forma un perfetto Prencipe, & una perfetta Republica e parimente un Senatore, un Cittadino, un Soldato, & un Mercatante* (Venice, 1563): "Benchè nella Republica Vinitiana *[sic]* sempre i mercatanti han governate et amministrate le cose publiche con gran prudenza. . . ." (Sig. H5). "In the second half of the *cinquecento* the Venetian merchant was already beginning to identify himself with the *cittadino*"—Ugo Tucci, "The Psychology of the Venetian Merchant in the Sixteenth Century" in Hale, ed., *Renaissance Venice*, p. 360.

9. ". . . per far mercatantia anchor si pèrda la nobiltà"—Muzio, *Il Gentilhuomo* (Venice, 1571), Sig. Q4v.

10. Cohen, p. 777.

11. Rose, p. 483. See also John C. Davis, *The Decline of the Venetian Nobility as a Ruling Class* (Baltimore: Johns Hopkins University Press, 1962).

12. Elze laboriously locates it in the neighborhood of Dolo (pp. 8–11).

13. Lloyd L. Mills goes so far as to suggest that Portia herself has secretly restored Antonio's fortune. See "Shakespearean Impudence: *The Merchant of Venice,* 5.1.273–79," *Neuphilologische Mitteilungen* 74 (1973): pp. 510–14.

14. Harley Granville-Barker, "The Merchant of Venice," in *Prefaces to Shakespeare,* 2 vols. (Princeton: Princeton University Press, 1946), I.335.

15. "The Jew as Stranger: or, 'These be the Christian husbands'" in *The Stranger in Shakespeare* (New York: Stein and Day, 1972), pp. 85–136, especially pp. 109–17.

16. See Draper, *The* Othello *of Shakespeare's Audience,* p. 18.

17. See, for instance, Guylforde, p. 9; Thomas, p. 69; Laurence Aldersey, "The first voyage . . . to the Cities of Jerusalem, and Tripolis . . . 1581" in *The Principall Navigations, Voiages and Discoveries of the English Nation* (1589), ed. Richard Hakluyt, Sig. P7; Moryson, I.192. Subsequent references to Aldersey will be included parenthetically in the text.

18. Pullan, *Listener,* p. 79.

19. *Delle cose notabili* 1587, Sig. 03v; Lewkenor, Sig. Bb3v. Modern historians place the figure higher. Pullan gives 1,694 in 1586; see *The Jews of Europe and the Inquisition of Venice, 1550–1670* (Oxford: Basil Blackwell, 1983), p. 156.

20. "Questi per il negotio, sono opulentissimi & ricchi, & dimorano più volentieri in Venetia ch'in altra parte d'Italia. Perciochè non si usano loro

violenze ne tirannidi come altrove, & sono sicuri in ogni occorrenza delle facultà loro . . . perciochè riposandosi in singolarissima pace, godono questa patria quasi come vera terra di promissione"—Sansovino, *Venetia,* 1581 ed., Sig. Mm.

21. *History,* pp. 116–120.

22. ". . . conseguiscono giustitia contra qualunque si sia"—1581 ed., Sig. Mm.

23. Roth says that in return for a certain amount of toleration many Venetian Jews were actually loyal to the Venetian state (p. 193).

24. Sansovino 1581, Sig. Mm; Aldersey, Sig. P7. Roth, *History,* notes that yellow was the earlier color and red the later, with a transition period (in the age of Shakespeare) between (p. 114).

25. M. Channing Linthicum, "My Jewish Gaberdine," *PMLA* 43 (1928): pp. 757–66.

26. Roth, p. 124.

27. Pullan, *Jews,* p. 158.

28. Roth, pp. 120–22.

29. ". . . acciochè le povere persone & le donne, non siano ingannate da i prestatori"—1581 ed., Sig. Mm. On the five percent interest, see Lane, p. 304. In contrast to the Jews of German origin, who were indeed moneylenders and pawnbrokers, there were a few privileged Levantine Jews in Venice in the 1590s who were permitted to trade with their homelands; these were the ones who grew truly rich and powerful. See Lane, p. 300 and Pullan, p. 568. Shakespeare can scarcely have known the fine distinctions between kinds of Jews.

30. "Hanno auttorità sopra i Giudei quando s'impacciono con Cristiane"—*Delle cose notabili* 1587, Sig. ɪ3.

31. Robert Withington, "Shakespeare and Race Prejudice" in *Elizabethan Studies and Other Essays in Honor of George F. Reynolds* (Boulder: University of Colorado Studies in the Humanities, vol. 2 (1945), pp. 172–84.

32. Lane, *Venice,* pp. 302–03. Pullan, *Rich and Poor,* p. 553, notes that in 1590 Jewish players got a license to play for Christians.

33. Pullan, *Jews,* p. 160ff.

34. The "tranect" (*Riverside,* 3.4.53) is usually emended by editors to "traject" and explained as referring to the thirteen "traghetti" which ferried people across canals in Venice. The theory is strengthened by the fact that at least one writer translating from Italian to Latin renders "traghetti" as "trajectus" (Vecellio 1598, Sig. P7). Caesar spells "transjectus," which might have been the source of Shakespeare's "n" (although the word in Latin means a crossing of a body of water, not a boat).

35. Thomas Wheeler, *The Merchant of Venice: An Annotated Bibliography* (New York: Garland, 1985), introduction, pp. xvi, xviii–xix.

Chapter 4. *Othello* and the Myth

1. Previous scholarship on the Venetian background of the play has devoted too much attention to the question of the *accuracy* of the Venetian local color. For instance, Thomas Rymer's famous diatribe contains the following: ". . . a body must strain hard to fancy the scene at Venice"—*A Short View of Tragedy,* 1693, in *The Critical Works of Thomas Rymer,* ed. Curt Zimansky (New Haven: Yale University Press, 1956), p. 138. In respect to the accuracy of the local color, Draper is a kind of latter-day Rymer; he spends most of his energy somewhat scornfully patronizing Shakespeare's *in*accuracies, and then (unlike

Rymer) concludes inexplicably that they do not really matter much after all; see *The* Othello *of Shakespeare's Audience,* p. 201. Because my interest is in the Myth, I largely ignore the whole question of accuracy.

A helpful study is Samuel Chew, *The Crescent and the Rose: Islam and England During the Renaissance* (1937; reprint, New York: Octagon, 1974). I admire W. H. Auden's understanding of the symbolic potential of Venice in the play, though my approach is quite different from his; see "The Alienated City: Reflections on *Othello,*" *Encounter* 17 (August 1961): pp. 3–14. For a psychological approach to the geographic shifts of scene in *Othello,* see Michael Neill, "Changing Places in *Othello,*" *ShS* 37 (1984): pp. 115–31.

2. Kernan, Introduction, Signet ed. (New York, 1963), pp. xxvi–xxxii.

3. Draper, "Shakespeare and the Doge of Venice," pp. 75–81.

4. See 1.1.29. Rhodes had actually been in Turkish hands since 1522, but Shakespeare's slight inaccuracy does not matter much in the context of my argument here.

5. Edwards, "A letter . . . written the 8. of August 1566 . . ." in *The Principall Navigations, Voiages and Discoveries of the English Nation* (1599), Sig. Gg6. Also, this: "The Venetians were far and away the leading Western merchants in Aleppo" (Lane, p. 304).

6. See Vecellio, 1590, Sigs. Qqq 6v–7. In a recent production by the Royal Shakespeare Company, Ben Kingsley played a distinctly Arabic Moor, turban and all. On the vexed question of whether Othello is to be thought of as an Arabic or Negroid Moor, see the following: Eldred Jones, *Othello's Countrymen* (London: Oxford University Press, 1965), pp. 120–25; Withington, "Shakespeare and Race Prejudice," pp. 172–84; Martin Orkin, "Othello and the 'plain face' of Racism," *SQ* 38 (1987): pp. 182–84.

7. The bow and arrows also appear in an engraving of a Moor by Boissard, *Habitus,* Plate 59. Violet M. Jeffery has argued that the Saggitary is a street, not an inn. See "Shakespeare's Venice," *MLR* 27 (1932): pp. 24–35.

8. Sig. S2v. Malone seems to have been the first to point out that this Venetian practice may relate to Othello; see *New Variorum,* I.iii.61n.

9. Again, Malone first pointed toward Lewkenor here (*Variorum,* I.i.200n). Lewkenor's Italian source, *Delle cose* (Sig. I3), specifies that the Officers of Night have it in their authority to punish "i rapitori, e corruttori delle donzelle" ("abductors and corrupters of maidens"), which is precisely the category that Brabantio believes that Othello falls into; but that idea did not make it into Lewkenor's English, and so the likelihood that Shakespeare knew about it is not very great.

10. Draper, *The* Othello *of Shakespeare's Audience,* p. 19.

11. Lane, p. 350.

12. See 2.1.43, 2.3.57.

13. Botero, *The Reason of State,* 1956 ed., p. 92.

14. The Furness *Variorum* cites Knolles, and Geoffrey Bullough accepts the book as a source—see VII. 262–65; but the best evidence is in Emrys Jones, "*Othello, Lepanto,* and the Cyprus Wars," *ShS* 21 (1968): pp. 47–52. Subsequent references to Knolles will be included parenthetically in the text.

15. Jones, p. 51.

16. Jones, p. 51.

17. *The Poems of James VI of Scotland,* ed. James Craigie. Scottish Text Society. (Edinburgh: William Blackwood, 1955), I.202.

18. Jones himself is an exception, however. Though far from making omi-

nousness his main point, he does observe: "The Turkish menace to Christendom was a fact of Shakespeare's entire lifetime. . . . This fact may of itself have given *Othello*'s Cypriot setting an ominous character which is lost on us" (p. 51).

19. Signet introduction, pp. xxv–xxvi.

20. Signet introduction, p. xxvi.

21. Othello *as the Tragedy of Italy* (London: T. Fisher Unwin, 1924).

22. Amelot, p. 266, cites Quintilian, who makes a roughly similar complaint about the morality of his own day. Ben Jonson also uses the Quintilian passage, with some updating: "Well, I thanke heaven, I never yet was he, / That travail'd with my sonne, before sixteene, / To shew him, the *Venetian cortezans*" (*Every Man in His Humour,* folio version, H&S 3, 2.5.44–46). See also St. Didier in English, Part III, p. 4.

23. *The* Othello *of Shakespeare's Audience,* p. 170.

24. Le Saige, *Voyage à Rome . . . Venise, Jerusalem. . . ,* ed. H. R. Duthilloeul (Douai, 1851): "Car les aultres jours tout du long de lannée elles sont en une chambre haulte. . . . Leurs maris en sont si jaloux quy ne les laissent point vuider" (p. 51).

25. I.403. Note that just as travelers' conceptions can influence playwrights, so playwrights can influence travelers' conceptions. Some of Coryat's observations about Venice make one wonder if he has not been to the Globe to see *Othello* (and *Volpone*) a few times.

26. *Shakespeare's Europe,* p. 152.

27. The translation is a shade more indignant than the original French, which reads: ". . . il y a même des maris, qui ayant quelque sujet d'en estre jaloux, les tiennent sans scruple les années entieres, sans les laisser sortir de leur maison" (*La Ville et la Republique de Venise,* Paris, 1680, p. 321). The word "prison" is the translator's (Part 3, p. 19).

28. Horatio Brown, *Studies in the History of Venice,* 2 vols. (London: John Murray, 1907), I.257.

29. "Un Sanudo che sta in rio della Croce alla Giudecca, *fece l'altro hieri confessare sua moglie* ch'era Cappello, et la notte seguente, su le cinque hore, li diede di un stiletto nella gola et la ammazzò: dicesi perchè non gli era fidele, ma la contrada la predica per una santa" (Italian from Molmenti, II.ii.172—translation mine).

30. Among the best known: F. R. Leavis, "Diabolic Intellect and the Noble Hero; or, the Sentimentalist's Othello," *Scrutiny* 6, no. 3 (December 1937); reprinted in F. R. Leavis, *The Common Pursuit* (London: Chatto and Windus, 1952), pp. 136–59.

31. Besides, we should perhaps think of Bianca as a Cypriot rather than a Venetian, though probably she followed Cassio to Cyprus.

32. ". . . pubbliche Meretrici condannate per trasgressioni alle Leggi"—Giovanni Battista Lorenzi, *Legge e memorie Venete sulla prostituzione fino alla caduta della Republica* (Venice, 1870–72), p. 15.

33. ". . . essendo communemente le Gentildonne Venetiane molto gelose dell'honor suo, & specchi d'honestà & di pudicitia"—1590 ed., Sig. S7.

34. Margaret L. King and Albert Rabil, Jr., eds. *Her Immaculate Hand: Selected Works by and About the Women Humanists of Quattrocento Italy.* Medieval and Renaissance Texts and Studies, 20 (Binghamton, N.Y.: Center for Medieval and Early Renaissance Studies, 1983).

35. King and Rabil, p. 17.

36. King and Rabil, p. 49.

37. Bandello, ed. Flora, I.155–82. For the French I have used *Le Troisiesme Tome . . . de Belleforest*, Sigs. a–g2. For Painter I quote from the ed. of Joseph Jacobs (London, 1890), III.125–56. Subsequent references will be included parenthetically in the text.

38. Bullough, I.274, Muir, *Sources*, p. 23.

39. The substance of her argument is like that of Emilia's; see 4.3.84–103.

40. Matt. xix.5, *King James Version*.

41. Douglas J. Stewart, "*Othello:* Roman Comedy as Nightmare," *Emory University Quarterly* 22 (1967): pp. 252–76; Barbara Heliodora C. de Mendonça, "*Othello:* A Tragedy Built on a Comic Structure," *ShS* 21 (1968): pp. 31–38; Susan Snyder, *The Comic Matrix of Shakespearean Tragedy* (Princeton: Princeton University Press, 1979), pp. 70–90; Francis Teague, "*Othello* and New Comedy," *Comparative Drama* 20 (1986): pp. 54–64.

Chapter 5. Theatricality and the Myth of Venice in *Volpone*

1. *Topographical Dictionary*, p. 543.

2. See, for example, the following: Richard Perkinson, "*Volpone* and the Reputation of Venetian Justice," *MLR* 35 (1940): pp. 11–18; Boughner, "Lewkenor and *Volpone*," already cited; C. J. Gianakaris, "Jonson's Use of 'Avocatori' in *Volpone*," *ELN* 12 (1974): pp. 8–14; Ralph Cohen, "The Setting of *Volpone*," *Renaissance Papers* (1978): pp. 65–75.

3. See Creaser ed. (London: Hodder and Stoughton, 1978). On Sir Politic and Lady Would-be, see introduction, pp. 45–59. See also Creaser's article, "A Vindication of Sir Politic Would-be," *English Studies* 57 (1976): pp. 502–14.

4. See Parker's introduction, pp. 19–22 and the excellent notes throughout, especially on Venetian local color. Parker's notes often go beyond the sterling work in the Herford and Simpson and Creaser editions. Also, he has kindly let me read in manuscript a forthcoming essay on Jonson's Venice in which he reaches the conclusion described.

5. Kernan, introduction, Yale ed. of *Volpone* (New Haven: Yale University Press, 1962), pp. 7–15. Perhaps even more important is Barish, *The Anti-Theatrical Prejudice* (Berkeley: University of California Press, 1981), pp. 132–54. For an earlier version, see Barish, "Jonson and the Loathèd Stage," in *A Celebration of Ben Jonson*, ed. William Blisset (Toronto: University of Toronto Press, 1973), pp. 27–53. Of lesser interest, but still very valuable, are the following: Stephen J. Greenblatt, "The False Ending in *Volpone*," *JEGP* 75 (1976): pp. 90–104; Alexander Leggatt, "The Suicide of Volpone," *UTQ* 39 (1969): pp. 19–32.

6. Thomas J. Greene, "Ben Jonson and the Centered Self," *SEL* 10 (1970): pp. 325–48.

7. I leave out of account the problem of theater as a medium (actors aping Britons aping Venetians aping Romans). The idea that Jonson's characters see themselves in flattering roles from literary works is used centrally by Robert N. Watson, *Ben Jonson's Parodic Strategy: Literary Imperialism in the Comedies* (Cambridge, Mass.: Harvard University Press, 1987), but he thinks Volpone sees himself as "the triumphant fox of the fable" (p. 88).

8. Muir, p. 68n.

9. Here is Scaliger's Latin text:

> Pervia Barbaricis tellus Oenotria turmis
> Pertulit impositi pondera dira jugi.

Ipsa suos flevit populares Roma Quirites:
Sensit & indomitae noxia tela manus.
Haud tulit hoc Genius, cujus fatalibus ausis
Tutior in medio Roma renata mari est.
Clara virûm virtus animo, insatiata cupido
Imperii, vastae non numerantur opes.
Juppiter, haud temerè tua sunt ita dissita coeli
Moenia, si possent tangere, parte cares.
(Quoted in Coryat, I.301)

10. Thomas de Fougasses, *The Generall Historie . . . of Venice*, Sig. A4.

11. Lithgow probably borrowed the image from Shute; it is not in Lithgow's 1614 version of his travels. Shute's translation was published in 1615, and Lithgow uses the metaphor in his 1623 version, Sig. D4v.

12. John Raymond, *An Itinerary Containing a Voyage Made through Italy in the Year 1646, and 1647* (London, 1648), Sig. ɪ10–ɪ10v. Raymond makes good use of a coincidence of chronology: the Roman Empire did indeed fall at about the time Venice was said to have been founded. Another comparison that stresses Rome because of its past and Venice because of its present is Botero, *Greatness of Cities*, 1956 ed., pp. 232–33.

13. *Suetonius*, trans. J. C. Rolfe, Loeb ed. (London: William Heinemann, 1913; reprint, 1964), Vol. ɪ, pp. 461–63. Volpone mentions exotic baths like Caligula's, 3.7.212–15; exotic foods, 201–04; pearls dissolved in vinegar, 190–92; and drink laced with gold, 216. Subsequent references to Suetonius will be included parenthetically in the text.

14. This flinging of gold from the balcony may have suggested to Stephan Zweig a similar action at the end of his adaptation of *Volpone;* but Zweig may instead (or also?) be borrowing from a Venetian custom that called for the Doge to fling money from his balcony on certain ceremonial occasions.

15. *Suetonius* ɪɪ.131–33. Lady Would-be mentions Sporus, *Volpone* 4.2.48.

16. See in Muir's bibliography, pp. 310–17, entries under the following names: Rocco Benedetti, Ioanne Planerio Quintiano Brixiensi, M. Pietro Buccio, Marsiglio Dalla Croce, Claudio Dorron, Luigi Groto, Nicolo Lucangeli da Bevagna, Dottore Manzini Bolognese (two pamphlets), Andrea Menechini, Octavianus Meninus; Francisci Morandi (two pamphlets); Bernardinus Parthenius Silimbergius.

17. ". . . le maggiori accoglienze che si vedessero giamai fatte da questo Stato. . ." and ". . . quanta sia la magnificenza de gli animi Vinitiani *[sic]*. . ." (1667 ed., p. 441). Sansovino's hyperboles are echoed by John Addington Symonds: "Venice, through those days of festival, exhibited the scene of one vast masque—the most imperially mounted and played on the most splendid theatre that earth can show"—*Shakespeare's Predecessors in the English Drama* (London, 1884), p. 335.

18. ". . . si spararono molti pezzi d'artigliaria, & si diede nelle trombe, & ne tamburi, sonandosi per tutto le Campane" (Sansovino, 1667 ed., p. 443).

19. "Questa galea fu la più bella che uscisse giamai dell'Arsenale" (p. 444).

20. ". . . trenta bandiere, alcune d'erminiso bianco, & turchino, & alcune di rosso, & giallo, con ricami d'oro, & d'argento col Leone del Vangelista nel mezzo. . ." (p. 444).

21. "Et quel che piu dava à ciascuno maraviglioso diletto, erano 354. Schiavoni

posti al remo, tutti vestiti di taffetta giallo, & panonazzo à livrea di esso Rè" (p. 444).

22. ". . . con un perpetuo tuono, & rimbombo d'artigliarie, di trombe, di tamburi, & di campane, che andavano al cielo. . ." (p. 445).

23. ". . . il Rè si pose su la finestra à vedere lo spettacolo maraviglioso della moltitudine delle barche . . . & del gran numero della gente, che stava su per le rive da un capo all'altro del Canal grande per le finestre, & per i tetti, à guardare. Ma cosa, sopra modo ammiranda, fu il vedere arder la notte lumi infiniti dall'una parte & dall'altra del sudetto canale: fatti diversamente in forma di gigli, di piramidi, di corone, & d'altre varie guise . . . cominciandosi da S. Marco fino à S. Lucia, che è lo spatio poco meno di due miglia. Et perchè tutti i lumi riflettevano nell'acqua con lo splendore, pareva che sotto il canale fosse un'altro cielo stellato. per lo qual tutta notte, molte gondole ripiene di ogni sorte di gente, andavano discorrendo a diporto" (pp. 445–46).

24. Sansovino was the son of the famous Florentine sculptor and architect Jacopo Sansovino, who designed the Marciana Library and other splendid Venetian buildings.

25. "Et non è possibile à fare in terra una rappresentatione più mirabile di quella. . ." (p. 446).

26. ". . . dugento gentildonne di singolar bellezza, tutte vestite di bianco, & adornate di perle, & d'infinite gioie di uno incredibil valore . . . passando di mano in mano dinanzi al Rè & inchinandoglisi. Et egli stette sempre con la berretta in mano. . . (p. 447).

27. ". . . confettioni di sessanta sorti, & con diverse statue, & figure di Zuccaro, di huomini, di Ninfe, di Lioni, di navi, di grifoni . . . trecento figure di Zuccaro, che per favore si dispensarono alle gentildonne. . . (p. 448).

28. ". . . l'apparecchio in quella gran Sala fu simile al convito de gli Dei figurato da i Poeti. . ." (p. 448)

29. Of the pamphlets listed by Muir (see note 16 above) half are in Latin. The festivities are also described in Latin in Franciscus Modius's *Pandectae Triumphales* (Frankfurt, 1586), Sigs. bb2–cc3. Jonson's own copy of this book at Clare College, Cambridge contains some of his most interesting marginalia; see H&S xi.594–96 and my catalogue of Jonson's library, p. 17 and pp. 71–72.

30. ". . . ita ut uniuscuiusque ornamentum quinquaginta millium aureorum precium excedere judicatum fuerit"—1598 ed., Sig. N5.

31. (". . . à contemplare il magnifico, & veramente maraviglioso theatro della città di Vinetia [*sic*]")—Porcacchi, *Le attioni d'Arrigo Terzo,* Sig. E4v.

32. Molmenti, II.ii.17.

33. Molmenti, II.ii.27.

34. See 1581 ed., Sig. Tt4v.

35. "Questi Comici Gelosi dunque rappresentarono al Rè una molto grata & gratiosa Tragicomedia, della qual sentì mirabil piacere: & ho inteso che gli recitarono ancho *[sic]* la Domenica sera, ch'ei fu venuto una Comedia: di che il Rè mostrò d'allegrarsi molto"—Porcacchi, Sig. G4.

36. ". . . recitar Comedie & far altri Spettacoli di grandissima spessa [*sic*]"—Vecellio 1590, Sig. F.

37. ". . . la quale averà ordinariamente sei or sette gentiluomini veneziani per suoi innamorati"—Bandello, *Tutte le Opere,* Part iii, Novella xxxi (Vol. ii, p. 418).

38. Hunter makes this point, *Dramatic Identities,* p. 23.

39. Herford and Simpson ed., II.50–54.
40. Leggatt, "Suicide," p. 20.
41. Petronius, trans. William Arrowsmith (New York: Mentor Books, 1959), p. 126. Arrowsmith's notes stress that the theatrical metaphor is in the Latin; see p. 184. Subsequent references to *The Satyricon* will be to this edition and will be included parenthetically in the text.
42. See, for example, *Suetonius* I.381; on eunuchs and hermaphrodites, see the references to Sporus, above.
43. Moryson, *Itinerary,* I.192: ". . . the Venetians being most sparing in diet and apparell. . . ."
44. See his edition of *Volpone* (New Haven: Yale University Press, 1919), p. 165.
45. Robert Knoll, *Ben Jonson: An Introduction* (Lincoln: University of Nebraska Press, 1964) pp. 82–89; R. B. Parker, "*Volpone* and *Reynard the Fox,*" *Renaissance Drama,* N.S. 7 (1976): pp. 3–42; Malcolm H. South, "Animal Imagery in *Volpone,*" *TSL* 10 (1965): pp. 141–50.
46. On Seneca and Martial, see note on the name *Voltore* in H&S IX.687; on Horace's legacy hunter as a "gaping raven" see *Horace: Satires, Epistles, Ars Poetica,* trans. H. R. Fairclough, Loeb ed. (London: William Heinemann, 1926; rpt. 1966), pp. 202–03.
47. George Parfitt notes that about 10 percent of the dialogue of the entire play is borrowed from the classics; see "Some Notes on the Classical Borrowings in *Volpone,*" *ES* 55 (1974): pp. 127–32. Another helpful study is James Riddell, "Seventeenth Century Identifications of Jonson's Sources in the Classics," *Renaissance Quarterly* 28 (1975): pp. 204–18.
48. Loeb ed., pp. 162–63.
49. On the famous carbuncle in the Treasury of St. Mark see Chapter 2. Jonson probably found out about the carbuncles by reading Aretino's *Il marescalco;* see Donaldson, pp. 139–40.
50. See H&S notes. The "by way of's" are obviously significant for my argument here. Jonson's marginalia seem to indicate that even when he reads Greek in a parallel Greek/Latin text, he checks his results by consulting the Latin as well; see my catalogue of his library, p. 18.
51. "Suicide," p. 22.
52. Craik, "Volpone's 'Young Antinöus,'" *N&Q* N.S. 17 (1970): pp. 213–14.
53. Simmons, "Volpone as Antinöus: Jonson and *Th'Overthrow of Stage-playes,*" *MLR* 70 (1975): pp. 13–19.
54. Fizdale, "Jonson's *Volpone* and the 'Real' Antinöus," *Renaissance Quarterly* 26 (1973): pp. 454–59. See also Michael J. Warren, "A Note on Jonson's *Volpone* 1.1.76–8," *N&Q,* N.S. 27 (1980): p. 144n.
55. Craik, "Volpone's 'young Antinöus' Again," *N&Q* 29 (1982): pp. 140–41, and Brooks-Davies, "Jonson's Volpone and Antinöus Once More," *N&Q,* N.S. 30 (1983): pp. 145–47.
56. Jonson in Herford and Simpson ed., VIII.638 (11.2469–73).
57. ". . . non solo del volto, ma di gran parte del petto imbiaccato & dipinto"—1590 ed., Sig. S8.
58. Several travel writers mention the sun hats with wide brim but no crown that permitted Venetian women to allow the sun to supplement chemical bleaches without sun-burning their faces; see, for instance, Coryat I.401.
59. Lines 17–18. "See" in 1.18 was "use" in Q, making the sexual pun even more obvious; Jonson probably decided to tone it down for F; see H&S note.

60. ". . . tiercement il n'y a point d'inquisition pour la foy, finalement chacun y vit à la fantasie & en liberté de conscience, qui est cause que plusiers Francois libertins y demeurent pour n'y estre recherchez & controollez [*sic*] & y vivre en toute licence, & grand nombre d'autres nations pour le plaisir qu'ils y ont chasque jour"—1600 ed., Sig. Ov.

61. Introduction to his ed., p. 46.

62. Besides Castiglione, see Botero: "Imperoche à una donna è supplitio così grave, come la morte ad un'huomo" ("For to a lady the loss of [sexual] honor is a punishment as grave as death to a man")—*Relatione della Republica Venetiana* (Venice, 1605), Sig. K7.

63. See in *BM Cat.* itself, but not in printed version thereof, under PIPPI (Guilio) *Romano. I sonnetti lussuriosi,* anno 1525 [Reproductions of a set of sixteen drawings by Pippi, illustrating the "Sonnetti lussuriosi." Preceded by a set of engravings after Pippi by Marc Antonio Raimondi. . . .] [Paris: Sybarite Club, 1905.]

On the possible influence of Aretino's bawdy writings on Jonson, see Neil Rhodes, *Elizabethan Grotesque* (London: Routledge & Kegan Paul, 1980), p. 134, 185.

64. *The Letters of John Chamberlain,* ed. Norman E. McClure. 2 vols. (Philadelphia: American Philosophical Society, 1939), I.302.

65. See 4.1.74–75 and Creaser's note thereon.

66. Horatio Brown, II.110–33.

67. To be fair to Sir Pol (and Lady Would-be), Mosca's lie would have had a certain plausibility; Molmenti says that "frequently the loose women of the town put on male attire" (II.ii.239).

68. Brown, II. 261.

69. Maurice Rowdon, *The Fall of Venice* (London: Weidenfeld and Nicolson, 1970), pp. 25–26.

70. Brown II.262.

71. Creaser, pp. 261–62.

72. Roger Ascham, *The Schoolmaster,* ed. Lawrence V. Ryan, Pub. for Folger Shakespeare Library. (Ithaca: Cornell University Press, 1967), p. 70.

73. 2.1.1. I owe these last two points, and many other excellent suggestions, to the reader's report forwarded to me by the University of Delaware Press.

74. Jonas Barish, "The Double Plot in *Volpone,*" *MP* 51 (1953): pp. 83–92; Creaser, introduction, pp. 58–59.

75. See, for instance, Parfitt, "Virtue and Pessimism in Three Plays by Ben Jonson," *Studies in the Literary Imagination* 6 (1973): pp. 23–40; Lawrence Levin, "Justice and Society in *Sejanus* and *Volpone,*" *Discourse* 13 (1970): pp. 319–24; Jay L. Halio, "Critical Introduction" to his edition of *Volpone* (Edinburgh: Oliver and Boyd, 1968), p. 6.

Conclusion: Shakespeare and Jonson Compared

1. Empson quoted by Gail Kern Paster, *The Idea of the City,* p. 4.

2. Cohen notes that the action is not only confined to Venice but to a rather small section of the city ("The Setting of Volpone," p. 70).

3. Laslett, *The World We Have Lost,* 2nd ed. (New York: Scribner's, 1971).

Works Cited

Abbot, George. *A Briefe Description of the Whole Worlde.* London, 1599.

———. *A Briefe Description of the Whole Worlde.* 2nd ed. London, 1599.

———. *A Briefe Description of the Whole Worlde.* 3rd ed. London, 1600.

———. *A Briefe Description of the Whole Worlde.* 4th ed. London, 1605.

Alberti, Leandro. *Descrittione di tutta Italia.* Venice, 1577.

Aldersey, Laurence, "The first voyage . . . to the Cities of Jerusalem, and Tripolis . . . 1581." In *The Principall Navigations, Voiages and Discoveries of the English Nation,* edited by Richard Hakluyt. London, 1589. Sigs. P5–Q2.

Amelot de la Houssaye, Abraham Nicholas. *Histoire du gouvernement de Venice.* Paris, 1676.

———. *The History of the Government of Venice.* Translator anonymous. London, 1677.

Arnold, Denis. "Venice." In *The New Grove Dictionary of Music and Musicians,* edited by Stanley Sadie, pp. 614–17. Vol. 19. London: Macmillan Co., 1980.

Ascham, Roger. *The Schoolmaster.* Edited by Lawrence V. Ryan. Published for The Folger Shakespeare Library. Ithaca: Cornell University Press, 1967.

Auden, W. H. "The Alienated City: Reflections on *Othello.*" *Encounter* (August 1961): pp. 3–14.

Avity, Pierre d'. *Les Empires, royaumes, estats, seigneuries, duchez, et principautez du monde.* St. Omer, 1614.

———. *The Estates, Empires, and Principallities of the World.* Translated by Edward Grimestone. London, 1614.

Bandello, Matteo. *Tutte le opere.* Edited by Francesco Flora. Milan: Mondadori, 1934–35.

———. *The Palace of Pleasure.* 3 vols. Translated by William Painter. Edited by Joseph Jacobs. 1566, 1575; 4th ed., London, 1890.

Bardi, Girolamo. *Dichiaratione di tutte le istorie, che si contengono nei quadri posti nuovamente nelle sali dello Scrutinio, & del Gran Consiglio, del Palagio Ducale.* Venice, 1587. Bound with Sansovino, *Delle cose,* for which Bardi is sometimes (probably erroneously) given credit.

Barish, Jonas. *The Anti-Theatrical Prejudice.* Berkeley: University of California Press, 1981.

———. "The Double Plot in *Volpone,*" *MP* 51 (1953): pp. 83–92.

———. "Jonson and the Loathèd Stage." In *A Celebration of Ben Jonson,* edited by William Blisset, pp. 27–53. Toronto: University of Toronto Press, 1973.

Bartlett, Kenneth R. "The Strangeness of Strangers: English Impressions of Italy in the Sixteenth Century." *Quaderni d'italianistica* 1 (1980): pp. 46–63.

Bates, E. S. *Touring in 1600: A Study in the Development of Travel as a Means of Education.* Boston: Houghton Mifflin, 1911.

Belleforest, Françoys de, trans. *Histoires tragiques, extraites de l'Italien de Bandel.* 7 vols. Paris, 1559–95.

Bembo, Pietro. *Della Historia Vinitiana* [*sic*]. Translated from Latin by Alemanio Fino. Venice, 1570.

Berveiller, M. "Influencias italianas en las comedias de Ben Jonson." *Filosofia y letras* 3 (1942): pp. 51–71.

Boccalini, Traiano. *De' Ragguagli di Parnaso.* Venice, 1612.

———. *I Ragguagli di Parnasso: or Advertisements from Parnassus.* Translated by Henry [Carey], Earl of Monmouth. London, 1656.

Bodin, Jean. *Les Six Livres de la Republique.* Paris, 1576.

———. *De Republica Libri Sex;* Latine ab Auctore Redditi. Frankfurt, 1591.

———. *Six Books of a Commonweal.* Translated by Richard Knolles. Edited by Kenneth D. McRae. London, 1606. Harvard Political Classics. Cambridge: Harvard University Press, 1962.

Boissard, Jean Jacques. *Habitus Variarum Orbis Gentium.* Mechlin (Belg.), 1581.

Boorde, Andrew. *The First Boke of the Introduction of Knowledge (1542).* Edited by F. J. Furnivall. Early English Text Society, Extra Ser. No. 10. London, 1870.

Botero, Giovanni. *Della ragion di stato.* Venice, 1589.

———. *The Reason of State.* Translated by P. J. and D. P. Waley. London: Routledge, 1956.

———. *Delle cause della grandezza della città.* Milan, 1596. Translated by Robert Peterson, London, 1606. Reprint. Edited by P. J. and D. P. Waley. London: Routledge, 1956.

———. *Relatione della republica Venetiana.* Venice, 1605.

———. *Relationi universali.* Vicenza, 1595–96. Translated by Robert Johnson. 3 eds.: *The Travellers Breviat.* London, 1601; *The Worlde.* London, 1601; *An Historicall Description.* London, 1603.

Boughner, Daniel. *The Devil's Disciple: Ben Jonson's Debt to Machiavelli.* New York: Philosophical Library, 1968.

———. "Lewkenor and *Volpone.*" *N&Q,* N.S. 9 (1962): pp. 124–30.

Braun, Georg and Frans Hogenberg. *Civitates Orbis Terrarum.* 5 vols. Cologne, 1572–98. Reprint. Cleveland: World Pub. Co., 1966. I.505.

Brook-Davies, Douglas, "Jonson's Volpone and Antinöus Once More." *N&Q,* N.S. 30 (1983): pp. 145–47.

Brown, Horatio F. *Studies in the History of Venice.* 2 vols. London: John Murray, 1907.

Bruyn, Abraham de. *Omnium pene Europae, Asiae, Aphricae atque Americae Gentium Habitus.* Antwerp, 1581.

Bullough, Geoffrey, ed. *Narrative and Dramatic Sources of Shakespeare.* 7 vols. London: Routledge, 1973.

Calendar of State Papers, Venetian. Vol. 9 (1591- 1603). Edited by Horatio F. Brown. Public Records Office. London: Her Majesty's Stationery Office, 1897.

Campbell, Oscar James. "The Relation of *Epicoene* to Aretino's *Il marescalco.*" *PMLA* 46 (1931): pp. 752–62.

——— and Edward Quinn, eds. *A Reader's Encyclopedia of Shakespeare*. New York: Crowell, 1966.

Casola, Pietro. *Canon Pietro Casola's Pilgrimage to Jerusalem in the Year 1494*. Edited and translated by M. Margaret Newett. Manchester: Manchester University Press, 1907.

Chamberlain, John. *Letters*. 2 vols. Edited by Norman E. McClure. Philadelphia: American Philosophical Society, 1939.

Chambrun, Clara Longworth de Pineton, Countess of. *Giovanni Florio: un apôtre de la Renaissance en Angleterre à lépoque de Shakespeare*. Paris: Payot, 1921.

Chew, Samuel. *The Crescent and the Rose: Islam and England During the Renaissance*. 1937. Reprint. New York: Octagon, 1974.

Cinthio, Giovanni Baptista. "The Moor of Venice." In *Hecatommithi* (Decade 3, no. 7). In *Shakespeare's Library*. 2d ed., rev. 6 vols. Edited by W. C. Hazlitt. 1875; rpt. New York: AMS Press, 1965. Section 1, Vol. 2: 285–308. Italian and English.

Cohen, Ralph. "The Setting of *Volpone*." *Renaissance Papers 1978*: pp. 65–75.

Cohen, Walter. "*The Merchant of Venice* and the Possibilities of Historical Criticism." *ELH* 49 (1982): pp. 765–89.

Colombo, Rosa Maria. "Venezia nel *Volpone* e nell'*Othello*." In *Shakespeare e Jonson: il teatro elisabettiano oggi*. Edited by Agostino Lombardo. Collana del teatro di Roma 8. Rome: Officina, 1979: pp. 95–111.

Comines, Philippe de. *Les Memoires*. Paris, 1593. Translated by Thomas Danett as *The Historie of Philip de Commines Knight, Lord of Argenton*. London, 1596.

Contarini, Gasparo. *De Magistratibus et Republica Venetorum*. Venice, 1589.

Coryat, Thomas. *Coryat's Crudities Hastily gobled up in five Moneths travells in France, Savoy, Italy* [etc.] (1611). 2 vols. Glasgow: James MacLehose, 1905.

Craik, T. W. "Volpone's 'Young Antinöus'." *N&Q*, N.S. 17 (1970): pp. 213–14.

———. "Volpone's 'young Antinöus' Again." *N&Q*, N.S. 29 (1982): pp. 140–41.

Creaser, John W. Introduction and notes to *Volpone*, by Ben Jonson. London: Hodder and Stoughton, 1978.

———. "A Vindication of Sir Politic Would-be." *English Studies* 57 (1976): pp. 502–14.

Crewe, J. V. "Death in Venice: A Study of *Othello* and *Volpone*." *University of Capetown Studies in English* 4 (1973): pp. 17–29.

Danson, Lawrence. *The Harmonies of* The Merchant of Venice. New Haven: Yale University Press, 1978.

Davis, John C. *The Decline of the Venetian Nobility as a Ruling Class*. Baltimore: Johns Hopkins University Press, 1962.

Donaldson, Ian. "Jonson's Italy: *Volpone* and Fr Thomas Wright." *N&Q*, N.S. 19 (1972), pp. 450–52.

———. "*Volpone* III.vii.193–4 and *Il marescalco*." *N&Q*, N.S. 29 (1982): pp. 139–40.

Draper, John W. *The* Othello *of Shakespeare's Audience*. 1952. Reprint. New York: Octagon, 1966.

———. "Shakespeare and the Doge of Venice." *JEGP* 46 (1947): pp. 75–81.

Edwards, Arthur. "A letter . . . written the 8. of August 1566. . ." In *The Principall Navigations, Voiages and Discoveries of the English Nation*, edited by Richard Hakluyt. London, 1599: Sigs. Gg5v–Hh.

Einstein, Lewis. *The Italian Renaissance in England.* New York: Columbia University Press, 1902.

Elze, Karl. *Essays on Shakespeare.* Translated by L. D. Schmitz. London, 1874.

Elze, Theodore. *Venezianische Skizzen.* Munich, 1899.

Engle, Lars. "'Thrift Is Blessing': Exchange and Explanation in *The Merchant of Venice.*" *SQ* 37 (1986): pp. 20–37.

Estienne, Henri. *Deux dialogues du nouveau langage françois italianizé.* Edited by Isidore Liseux. Paris, 1883.

Fellheimer, Jeannette. "The Englishman's Conception of the Italian in the Age of Shakespeare." Thesis. London University, 1935.

Fenton, Geoffrey, trans. *Tragical Tales,* by Matteo Bandello. 1567. Edited by Hugh Harris. Broadway Translations. London: Routledge, 1924.

Ferrara, Fernando. *Shakespeare e la commedia.* Bari: Adriatica Editrice, 1964.

Fiedler, Leslie. "The Jew as Stranger: or, 'These be the Christian husbands.'" In *The Stranger in Shakespeare.* New York: Stein and Day, 1972: pp. 85–136.

Fink, Zera S. *The Classical Republicans: An Essay in the Recovery of a Pattern of Thought in Seventeenth Century England.* Northwestern University Studies in the Humanities, No. 9. Evanston, Ill.: Northwestern University Press, 1945.

Finlay, Robert. *Politics in Renaissance Venice.* London: Ernest Benn, 1980.

Fizdale, Tay. "Jonson's *Volpone* and the 'Real' Antinöus." *Renaissance Quarterly* 26 (1973): pp. 454–59.

Florio, John. *Florio his firste Fruites: which yeelde familiar speech, merie Proverbes, wittie sentences, and golden sayings. Also a perfect Induction to the Italian, and English tongues.* London, 1578.

———. *Florio's Second Frutes . . . To which is annexed his Gardine of Recreation, yeelding six thousand Italian Proverbs.* London, 1591.

———. *A Worlde of Wordes.* London, 1598. Reprint facsimile. Hildesheim: Georg Olms Verlag, 1972.

Fougasses, Thomas de. *See under* Shute, W.

Fox (servant to Henry Cavendish). *Mr. Harrie Cavendish His Journey to and from Constantynople, 1589.* Edited by A. C. Wood. Camden Miscellany, XVII, Part 2. Third Series, 64. London: Royal Historical Society, 1940.

Franco, Giacomo. *Habiti d'huomeni* [*sic*] *et donne Venetiane.* Venice, ca. 1609.

Furness, Howard H., ed. *The Merchant of Venice.* New Variorum. 3d ed. Philadelphia, 1888.

———, ed. *Othello.* New Variorum. 3d ed. Philadelphia, 1886.

Gaeta, Franco. "Alcuni considerazioni sul mito di Venezia." *Bibliothèque d'humanisme et Renaissance* 23 (1961): pp. 58–75.

Gianakaris, C. J. "Jonson's Use of 'Avocatori' in *Volpone.*" *ELN* 12 (1974): pp. 8–14.

Giannotti, Donato. *Della republica et magistrati di Venetia.* Venice, 1591.

Giovanni, Ser, Fiorentino. "The Adventures of Giannetto" from *Il pecorone.* In *Shakespeare's Library,* edited by W. C. Hazlitt, section 1, vol. 1, 319–53. 2d ed., rev. 6 vols. 1875. Reprint. New York: AMS Press, 1965. Italian and English.

Giovio, Paolo. *Delle istorie del suo tempo.* Venice, 1565.

Gotch, J. Alfred. *Inigo Jones.* London: Methuen, 1928.

Granville-Barker, Harley. "The Merchant of Venice." In *Preface to Shakespeare,* 335–66. 2 vols. Princeton: Princeton University Press, 1946.

Greenblatt, Stephen J. "The False Ending in *Volpone.*" *JEGP* 75 (1976): pp. 90–104.

Greene, Thomas J. "Ben Jonson and the Centered Self." *SEL* 10 (1970): pp. 325–48.

Guicciardini, Francesco. *The Historie of Italie.* Translated by Geoffrey Fenton. London, 1579. 2d ed. London, 1599.

Guylforde, Sir Richard. *The pylgrymage of Sir Richard Guylforde to the Holy Land,* A.D. 1506. 1511. London: Camden Society, 1851.

Hale, John R. *England and the Italian Renaissance.* London: Faber and Faber, 1954.

———, ed. *Renaissance Venice.* London: Faber and Faber, 1973.

Halio, Jay L. "Critical Introduction" to his edition of Ben Jonson's *Volpone.* Edinburgh: Oliver and Boyd, 1968, pp. 1–6.

Harris, John, ed. *Navigantium atque Itinerantium Biblioteca.* London, 1705.

Herford, C. H., Percy Simpson, and Evelyn Simpson, eds. *See under* Jonson, Ben.

Hoby, Thomas. *The Travels and Life of Sir Thomas Hoby . . . Written by Himself. 1547–1564,* edited by Edgar Powell. Camden Miscellany, x, Part 2. Camden Third Series, iv. London: Royal Historical Society, 1902.

Hodge, Nancy Elizabeth. "Shakespeare's Merchant and His Venice: Setting Antonio to Scale in His Proper World." Diss. Vanderbilt University, 1984.

Horace [Quintus Horatius Flaccus]. *Satires, Epistles and Ars Poetica.* Edited and translated by H. Rushton Fairclough. Loeb edition. London: William Heinemann, 1926. Reprint, 1966.

Howell, James. *S.PQ.V.: A Survay of the Signorie of Venice.* London, 1651.

Hunter, G. K. *Dramatic Identities and Cultural Tradition: Studies in Shakespeare and His Contemporaries.* Liverpool: Liverpool University Press, 1978.

Hurrell, John D. "Love and Friendship in *The Merchant of Venice.*" *TSLL* 3 (1961): pp. 328–41.

Jacob, Cary F. "Reality and *The Merchant of Venice.*" *Quarterly Journal of Speech* 28 (1942): pp. 307–15.

James vi, King of Scotland. "Lepanto." In *Poems,* edited by James Craighie, i.197–257. 2 vols. Scottish Text Society. Edinburgh: William Blackwood, 1955.

Jeffery, Violet M. "Shakespeare's Venice." *MLR* 27 (1932): pp. 24–35.

Jones, Eldred. *Othello's Countrymen.* London: Oxford University Press, 1965.

Jones, Emrys. "*Othello, Lepanto,* and the Cyprus Wars." *ShS* 21 (1968): pp. 47–52.

Jonson, Ben. *Ben Jonson.* Edited by C. H. Herford, Percy Simpson, and Evelyn Simpson. 11 vols. Oxford: Clarendon Press, 1925–52.

———. *Volpone.* Edited by R. B. Parker. Revels edition. Manchester: Manchester University Press, 1983.

Kernan, Alvin. Introduction to *Othello,* by William Shakespeare, pp. xxiii–xxxv. Signet Classic. New York: New American Library, 1963.

———, ed. *Volpone,* by Ben Jonson. The Yale Ben Jonson. New Haven: Yale University Press, 1962.

King, Margaret L. *Venetian Humanism in an Age of Patrician Dominance.* Princeton: Princeton University Press, 1986.

King, Margaret L. and Albert Rabil, Jr., eds. *Her Immaculate Hand: Selected Works by and about the Women Humanists of Quattrocento Italy.* Medieval and Renaissance Texts and Studies, 20. Binghamton, N.Y.: Center for Medieval and Early Renaissance Studies, 1983.

Knoll, Robert. *Ben Jonson: An Introduction.* Lincoln: University of Nebraska Press, 1964.

Knolles, Richard. *The Generall Historie of the Turkes.* London, 1603.

Labalme, Patricia. *Bernardo Giustiniani: A Venetian of the Quattrocento.* Rome: Edizioni di storie e letteratura, 1969.

La Boetie, Etienne. *Anti-Dictator.* Translated by Harry Kurz. New York: Columbia University Press, 1942.

Lambin, Georges. *Voyages de Shakespeare en France et en Italie.* Geneva: Droz, 1962.

Lane, Frederick C. *Venice: A Maritime Republic.* Baltimore: Johns Hopkins University Press, 1973.

Laslett, Peter. *The World We Have Lost.* 2d ed. New York: Scribner's, 1971.

Lassels, Richard. *The Voyage to Italy.* Paris, 1670.

Leavis, F. R. "Diabolic Intellect and the Noble Hero; Or, the Sentimentalist's Othello." *Scrutiny* (1937). Reprinted in Leavis, *The Common Pursuit,* pp. 136–59. London: Chatto and Windus, 1952.

LeFranc, Abel. *A la découverte de Shakespeare.* Paris: Michel, 1950.

Leggatt, Alexander. "The Suicide of Volpone." *UTQ* 39 (1969): pp. 19–32.

Le Saige, Jacques. *Voyage à Rome, Notre-Dame-de-Lorette, Venise, Jerusalem et autres Saints lieux.* Edited by H. R. Duthilloeul. Douai, 1851.

Levin, Lawrence. "Justice and Society in *Sejanus* and *Volpone.*" *Discourse* 13 (1970): pp. 319–24.

Levith, Murray J. *Shakespeare's Italian Settings and Plays.* New York: St. Martin's Press, 1989.

Lewkenor, Lewis. *The Commonwealth and Government of Venice.* In part translated from Gasparo Contarini, *De Magistratibus et Republica Venetorum* (1543). London, 1599.

———. *The Estate of English Fugitives Under the King of Spain.* London, 1595.

———, trans. *The Resolved Gentleman,* by Olivier de la Marche. London, 1594.

Lewkenor, Samuel. *A Discourse of . . . Citties wherein doe flourish . . . priviledged Universities.* London, 1600.

Lievsay, John. *The Elizabethan Image of Italy.* Published for The Folger Shakespeare Library. Ithaca: Cornell University Press, 1964.

———. *Venetian Phoenix: Paolo Sarpi.* Lawrence: University of Kansas Press, 1973.

Limojon de Saint Didier, Alexandre Toussaint. *La Ville et la republique de Venise.* Paris, 1680.

———. *The City and Republick of Venice.* Translator anonymous. London, 1699.

Linthicum, M. Channing. *Costume in the Drama of Shakespeare and His Contemporaries.* Oxford: Claredon Press, 1936.

———. "My Jewish Gaberdine." *PMLA* 43 (1928): pp. 757–66.

Lipsius, Justus. Letter to Philip Lanoy, 1578. In *Epistolarum Centuriae Duae* (Frankfurt, 1591), Centuria I., Epist. xxii, Sig. C4-C7v. Translated by Sir John Stradling as *A Direction for Travailers.* London, 1592.

Lithgow, William. *A Most Delectable, and True Discourse, of an admired and painefull peregrination.* London, 1614. Another ed., augmented. London, 1623.

———. *The Total Discourse of the Rare Adventures and Painefull Peregrinations,* 1632. Glasgow: James MacLehose, 1906.

Logan, Oliver. *Culture and Society in Venice, 1470–1740.* London: B. T. Batsford, 1972.

Lorenzi, Giovanni Battista. *Legge e memorie Venete sulla prostituzione fino alla caduta della republica.* Venice, 1870–72.

Machiavelli, Nicolò. *Chief Works, and Others.* 3 vols. Translated by Allen Gilbert. Durham, N.C.: Duke University Press, 1965.

Mallet, M. F. and J. R. Hale. *The Military Organization of a Renaissance State: Venice c. 1400 to 1617.* Cambridge: Cambridge University Press, 1984.

Marlowe, Christopher. *The Jew of Malta.* Edited by Richard Van Fossen. Bison. Lincoln: University of Nebraska Press, 1964.

Martinengo, Nestore. *The true Report of all the successe of Famagosta.* Translated by William Malim. London, 1572.

Matchett, William. "Shylock, Iago, and Sir Thomas More: With Further Discussion of Shakespeare's Imagination." *PMLA* 92 (1977): pp. 217–30.

Maugham, Henry Neville. *The Book of Italian Travel (1580–1900).* London: Grant Richards, 1903.

McPherson, David. *Ben Jonson's Library and Marginalia. SP,* Texts and Studies Issue, 71 (1974).

———. "Lewkenor's Venice and Its Sources." *Renaissance Quarterly* 42 (1988): pp. 459–66.

McNeill, William H. *Venice: the Hinge of Europe, 1081–1797.* Chicago: University of Chicago Press, 1974.

McWilliam, George W. *Shakespeare's Italy Revisited.* Leicester: Leicester University Press, 1974.

Memmo, Giovanni Maria. *Dialogo . . . nel quale . . . si forma un perfetto prencipe, & una perfetta republica e parimente un senatore, un soldato, & un mercatante.* Venice, 1563.

Mendonça, Barbara Heliodora C. de. "*Othello:* A Tragedy Built on a Comic Structure." *ShS* 21 (1968): pp. 31–38.

Midgley, Graham. "*The Merchant of Venice:* A Reconsideration." *EIC* 10 (1960): pp. 119–31.

Mills, Lloyd L. "Shakespearean Impudence: *The Merchant of Venice* v,i, 273–279." *Neuphilologische Mitteilungen* 74 (1973): pp. 510–14.

Modius, Franciscus. *Pandectae Triumphales.* Frankfurt, 1586.

Molmenti, Pompeo. *Venice: Its Individual Growth from Earliest Beginnings to the Fall of the Republic.* Part II: The Golden Age. 2 vols. Translated by Horatio F. Brown. London: John Murray; Chicago: A. C. McClurg, 1907.

Montaigne, Michel de. *The Diary of Montaigne's Journey to Italy in 1580 and 1581.* Translated by E. J. Trechmann. London: Leonard and Virginia Woolf, 1929.

Moryson, Fynes. *An Itinerary Containing His Ten Yeares Travell* . . . 4 vols. 1617. Glasgow: James MacLehose, 1907.

———. *Shakespeare's Europe.* Edited by Charles Hughes. 1903. Reprint. New York: Benjamin Blom, 1967.

Muir, Edward. *Civil Ritual in Renaissance Venice.* Princeton: Princeton University Press, 1981.

Muir, Kenneth. "Shakespeare and Lewkenor." *RES* 7 (1956): pp. 182–83.

———. *Shakespeare's Sources.* London: Methuen, 1957.

Mulier, Eco O. G. Haitsma. *The Myth of Venice and Dutch Republican Thought in the Seventeenth Century.* Translated by Gerald T. Moran. Assen, The Netherlands: Van Gorcum, 1980.

Münster, Sebastian. *Cosmographiae Universalia Lib.* VI (Basel, 1550).

Muzio, Girolamo. *Il gentilhuomo.* Venice, 1571.

Neill, Michael. "Changing Places in *Othello.*" *ShS* 37 (1984): pp. 115–31.

Orkin, Martin. "*Othello* and the 'plain face' of Racism." *SQ* 38 (1987): pp. 166–88.

Ovid [Publius Ovidius Naso]. *Fasti.* Translated and edited by James G. Frazer. Loeb edition. London: William Heinemann, 1931.

Painter, William, trans. *The Palace of Pleasure,* by Matteo Bandello. 4th ed. 3 vols. Edited by Joseph Jacobs. 1566, 1575. London, 1890.

Parfitt, George. "Some Notes on the Classical Borrowings in *Volpone.*" *ES* 55 (1974): pp. 127–32.

———. "Virtue and Pessimism in Three Plays by Ben Jonson." *Studies in the Literary Imagination* 6 (1973): pp. 23–40.

Parker, R. B. "*Volpone* and *Reynard the Fox.*" *Renaissance Drama,* N.S. 7 (1976): pp. 3–42.

Parker, R. B., ed. *See under* Jonson, Ben: *Volpone.*

Parks, George B. *See under* Thomas, William.

Partridge, A. C. "Shakespeare and Italy." *English Studies in Africa* 4 (1961): pp. 117–27.

Paruta, Paolo. *Discorsi politici.* Venice, 1599. Translated by Henry [Carey], Earl of Monmouth. London, 1657.

———. *The History of Venice.* 1605. Translated by Henry [Carey], Earl of Monmouth. 1605. London, 1658.

Paster, Gail Kern. *The Idea of the City in the Age of Shakespeare.* Athens: University of Georgia Press, 1985.

Perkinson, Richard. "*Volpone* and the Reputation of Venetian Justice." *MLR* 35 (1940): pp. 11–18.

Petronius, Gaius. *The Satyricon.* Translated by William Arrowsmith. Mentor. New York: New American Library, 1959.

Philalethes, Polytopiensi [pseud. Ortensio Landi or Lando]. *Forcianae Quaestiones.* [Naples, 1536].

Piccolomini, Alessandro, Pius II. *Memoirs of a Renaissance Pope: The Commentaries of Pius* II. An Abridgement. Edited by Leona C. Gabel. Translated by Florence A. Gragg. London: George Allen & Unwin, 1960.

Pighius, Stephanus. *Hercules Prodicius.* Antwerp, 1587.

Pippi, Giulio, *Romano. I sonnetti lussuriosi.* Anno 1525 [. . . Without text.] [Paris: Sybarite Club, 1905.]

Pius II, Pope. *See under* Piccolomini, Alessandro.

Pocock, J. G. A. *The Machiavellian Moment: Florentine Political Thought and the Atlantic Republican Tradition.* Princeton: Princeton University Press, 1975.

Porcacchi, Tommasso. *Le attioni d'Arrigo Terzo Rè di Francia . . . descritte in dialogo.* Venice, 1574.

Praz, Mario. *The Flaming Heart.* 1958. Reprint. Gloucester, Mass.: Peter Smith, 1966.

———. "Italy." In *A Reader's Encyclopedia of Shakespeare,* edited by Oscar James Campbell and Edward Quinn, pp. 390–93. New York: Crowell, 1966.

Pullan, Brian. *The Jews of Europe and the Inquisition of Venice, 1550–1670.* Oxford: Basil Blackwell, 1983.

———. *Rich and Poor in Renaissance Venice.* Oxford: Basil Blackwell, 1971.

———. "Shakespeare's Venice." *Listener* 18 (January 1973): pp. 79–82.

———. Introduction to Alberto Tenenti, *Piracy and the Decline of Venice,* 1580–1615, translated by Janet and Brian Pullan. London: Longman's, 1967.

Queller, Donald. *The Venetian Patriciate: Reality vs. Myth.* Urbana: University of Illinois Press, 1986.

Ravà, Beatrix. *Venise dans la littérature française depuis les origines jusqu'à la mort de Henry* IV. Paris: Edoard Champion, 1916.

Raymond, John. *An Itinerary Containing a Voyage Made through Italy in the Year 1646, and 1647.* London, 1648.

Rea, John D. Introduction and notes to *Volpone,* by Ben Jonson. New Haven: Yale University Press, 1919.

Rébora, Piero. *L'Italia nel dramma inglese (1558–1642).* Milan: "Modernissima," 1925.

Rhodes, Neil. *Elizabethan Grotesque.* London: Routledge & Kegan Paul, 1980.

Riddell, James. "Seventeenth Century Identifications of Jonson's Sources in the Classics." *Renaissance Quarterly* 28 (1975): pp. 204–18.

Rose, Charles J. "Marc [*sic*] Antonio Venier, Renier Zeno and 'The Myth of Venice.'" *The Historian* 36 (1974): pp. 479–97.

Rossi, Sergio. "Note sugli Italiani in Inghilterra nell'età del Rinascimento." In *Saggi sul Rinascimento,* edited by Sergio Rossi, pp. 55–115. Biblioteca de Anglistica: Collano de testi e studi, vol. I. Milan: Edizioni Unicolpi, 1984.

———. *Richerche sull'Umanismo e sul Rinascimento in Inghilterra.* Milan: Vita e pensiero, 1969.

Roth, Cecil. "The Background of Shylock." *RES* 9 (1933): pp. 148–56.

———. *History of the Jews in Venice.* 1930. Reprint. New York: Schocken, 1975.

Rowden, Maurice. *The Fall of Venice.* London: Weidenfeld and Nicolson, 1970.

Rymer, Thomas. *A Short View of Tragedy.* In *Critical Works,* edited by Curt Zimansky, pp. 82–175. New Haven: Yale University Press, 1956.

Saint Didier. *See under* Limojon de Saint Didier, Alexandre Toussaint.

Sansovino, Francesco. *Delle cose notabili della città di Venetia.* Venice, 1587. Sometimes listed (probably erroneously) as by Girolamo Bardi.

———. *Ritratto delle più nobili et famose città d'Italia.* Venice, 1575.

———. *Venetia città nobilissima.* Venice, 1581. Another ed., augmented. Venice, 1604. Another ed., augmented. Venice, 1667. Reprint facsimile of 1667 ed. Edited by Jennifer M. Fletcher. Farnborough, Hants.: Gregg International, 1968.

Schoenbaum, Samuel. *Shakespeare: A Documentary Life.* New York: Oxford University Press, 1975.

Schott, Franciscus. *Itinerarii Italiae.* Antwerp, 1600.

———. *Itinerary.* Translated by Edmond Warcupp. London, 1660.

Shakespeare, William. *The Riverside Shakespeare.* Edited by G. Blakemore Evans et al. Boston: Houghton Mifflin, 1974.

Shute, W. "To the Reader." In his translation of Thomas de Fougasses, *The General Historie of the Magnificent State of Venice,* Sigs. A3–A3v. London, 1612.

Sidney, Sir Philip. *The Correspondence of Sir Philip Sidney and Hubert Languet.* Edited and translated by Steuart A. Pears. London, 1845.

Simmons, J. L. "Volpone as Antinöus: Jonson and *Th'Overthrow of Stage-playes.*" *MLR* 70 (1975): pp. 13–19.

Simonini, R. C., Jr. "Italian-English Language Books of the Renaissance." *Romanic Review* 42 (1951): pp. 241–44.

Smith, Logan Pearsall. *The Life and Letters of Sir Henry Wotton.* 2 vols. Oxford: Clarendon Press, 1907. Reprinted 1966.

Snyder, Susan. *The Comic Matrix of Shakespearean Tragedy.* Princeton: Princeton University Press, 1979.

South, Malcolm H. "Animal Imagery in *Volpone.*" *TSL* 10 (1965): pp. 141–50.

Stewart, Douglas J. "*Othello:* Roman Comedy as Nightmare." *Emory University Quarterly* 22 (1967): pp. 252–76.

Stoye, John Walter. *English Travellers Abroad, 1604–1667: Their Influence in English Society and Politics.* London: Jonathan Cape, 1952.

Suetonius [Gaius Suetonius Tranquillus]. *Lives of the Caesars.* 2 vols. Edited and translated by J. C. Rolfe. Loeb edition. London: William Heinemann, 1913; Reprinted 1964.

Sugden, Edward. *A Topographical Dictionary to the Works of Shakespeare and His Fellow Dramatists.* London: Longmans, Green, 1925.

Symonds, John Addington. *Shakespeare's Predecessors in the English Drama.* London, 1884.

Teague, Francis. "*Othello* and New Comedy." *Comparative Drama* 20 (1986): pp. 54–64.

Tenenti, Alberto. *See under* Pullan, Brian.

Thomas, William. *The History of Italy.* Edited by George B. Parks. Published for The Folger Shakespeare Library. Ithaca: Cornell University Press, 1963.

Torkington, Richard. *Ye Oldest Diarie of Englysshe Travell: Sir Richard Torkington . . . 1517.* Edited by W. J. Loftie. London, ca. 1880.

Tucci, Ugo. "The Psychology of the Venetian Merchant in the Sixteenth Century." In *Renaissance Venice,* edited by John R. Hale, 346–78. London: Faber and Faber, 1973.

Tyson, Brian. "Ben Jonson's Black Comedy: A Connection Between *Othello* and *Volpone.*" *SQ* 29 (1978): pp. 60–66.

Vecellio, Cesare. *De gli habiti antichi, et moderni di diverse parti del mondo.* Venice, 1590.

———. [Another ed.]. *De gli habiti antichi, et moderni di tutto il mundo.* Venice, 1598. Text in Italian, Latin.

———. [Another ed.]. *Costumes anciens et modernes.* 2 vols. Paris, 1859–60. Abbreviated text in Italian, French.

———. [Another ed.]. *Vecellio's Renaissance Costume Book: All 500 Woodcut Illustrations from the Famous Sixteenth-Century Compendium of World Costume.* New York: Dover, 1977. Text (captions only) in English.

Villamont, Jacques de. *Les Voyages du seigneur de Villamont.* Arras, 1598. Paris, 1600.

Warren, Michael J. "A Note on Jonson's *Volpone* I.i.76–8." *N&Q,* N.S. 27 (1980): pp. 143–46.

Watson, Robert N. *Ben Jonson's Parodic Strategy: Literary Imperialism in the Comedies.* Cambridge: Harvard University Press, 1987.

Webbe, Edward. *The Rare . . . things which Edw. Webbe hath seene . . . in the Gallies . . . of the great Turke.* London, 1590.

Weigel, Hans. *Habitus Praecipuorum Populorum.* Nuremberg, 1577.

Wheeler, Thomas, ed. Introduction. *The Merchant of Venice: An Annotated Bibliography,* xi–xxii. New York: Garland, 1985.

Whitfield, Christopher. "Sir Lewis Lewkenor and *The Merchant of Venice:* A Suggested Connexion." *N&Q,* N.S. 11 (1964): pp. 123–33.

Wilson, F. P. "Shakespeare's Reading." *ShS* 3 (1950): pp. 14–21.

Wilson, Milton. "Travellers' Venice: Some Images for Byron and Shelley." *UTQ,* 43 (1974): pp. 93–120.

Winstanley, Lillian. Othello *as the Tragedy of Italy.* London: T. Fisher Unwin, 1924.

Withington, Robert. "Shakespeare and Race Prejudice." In *Elizabethan Studies and Other Essays in Honor of George F. Reynolds,* pp. 172–84. University of Colorado Studies. Series B.: Studies in the Humanities, Vol. 2, no. 4. Boulder: University of Colorado Press, 1945.

Wordsworth, William. *Complete Poetical Works.* Cambridge edition. Boston: Houghton Mifflin, 1932.

Yates, Frances. *John Florio: The Life of an Italian in Shakespeare's England.* Cambridge: Cambridge University Press, 1934.

———. *A Study of* Love's Labour's Lost. Shakespeare Problem Series, 5. Cambridge: Cambridge University Press, 1936.

Zaltieri, Bolognino. Map of Venice ("Venetia ex aeneis formis Bolognini Zaltierii"). British Museum Pressmark: Maps C.7.e.2, Map. No. 66. Venice, 1566. Reprinted in Braun and Hogenberg, *Civitates Orbis Terrarum.*

Index